INSIGHT POCKET GUIDES

PaRIS

W9-BSQ-321

APA PUBLICATIONS

Part of the Langenscheidt Publishing Group

L

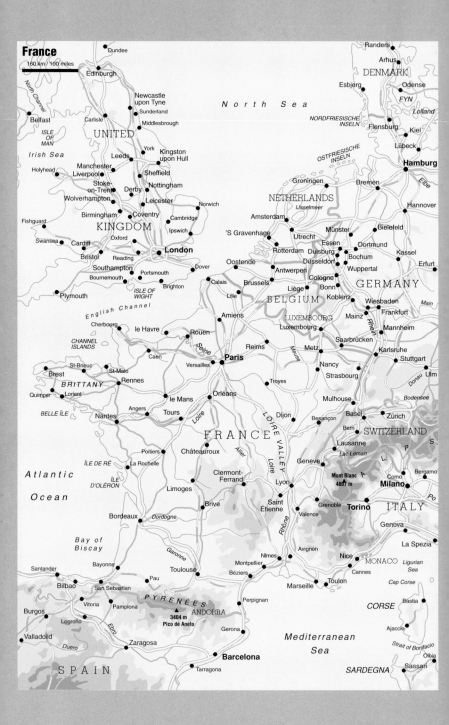

Welcome!

Besides being perhaps the best preserved and grandest city in the world, Paris is a major hub of intellectual, cultural and artistic pursuits. It is loved universally for its cuisine, wine, fashion, painting, theatre and museums. 'If a man fell out of the moon into the town of Paris,' said G. K. Chesterton in 1908, 'he would know that it was the capital of a great nation.'

 Grace Coston, our correspondent in the city, is not from the moon but from America. 'Even after 10 years here I am still discovering more about Paris every day,' she says. Grace has worked here as a writer, translator, teacher, and now mother to bilingual children. 'I can firmly say that I wouldn't live anywhere else, and my enthusiasm for the city is even greater than it was when I first arrived.'

Grace's enthusiasm for Paris, combined with her writer's instincts and outsider's eye, makes her an ideal correspondent for Insight Guides. Her enthusiasm illuminates her carefully-devised itineraries that fill the main part of this book. These routes include all the essential sights, as well as Grace's own favourite corners of what is a fairly compact city. Each has Grace's own personal selection of cafés and restaurants.

In addition, she has created four day-trips to well-known destinations such as Versailles and Euro Disneyland, and to less visited ones such as Monet's house and garden in Normandy. 'This book is a way of showing off my home town,' says Grace. 'And any friend of Paris is a friend of mine.'

So welcome to Paris – and let Grace show you the best of the city.

C O N T E N T S

Pages 2/3:
Eiffel Tower
from
Trocadéro

BASTILLE

4 Montmartre and Pigalle leads you up this legendary hill to *Sacré Coeur* and the *Place du Tertre*. Find the *Dali* collection and the *Montmartre Museum*, then head down for nightlife at the Place de Clichy, Pigalle and the *Moulin Rouge*

5 By Canal to La Villette, a boat trip, passes under *Bastille* and along canals to *Parc de la Villette*, home of the *City of Science and Industry*, a museum popular with children

6 The New Louvre is a brief guide to this superb, recently-reorganised museum

7 La Défense is a highly recommended visit to this avant-garde business district on the west side of the centre

Excursions

Four trips head out in all directions. *Versailles* includes a tour of the fabulous palace and gardens created by the Sun King Louis XIV; *Chartres* has one of the world's finest Gothic cathedrals; *Giverny* was home to Monet and includes the gardens depicted in so many of his paintings; *Euro Disneyland* is a slice of America at Marne la Vallée near Paris. These trips are ideal for weekends

Pages 8/9:
Looking down on
the Seine

Shopping, Dining & Nightlife

In this back section of the book are ideas on what to eat and what to buy in Paris, including recommended shops, restaurants and nightclubs

Calendar of Events

A listing of what's worth watching out for in a Parisian year

Practical Information

All the essential background information for your visit to Paris, from taxis to tipping, customs to consulates. The section includes a discriminating list of recommended hotels

Maps

HISTORY &

From Mud Huts to Palaces

Long ago, Paris was a simple village of mud huts nestled on an island in the river Seine. At the far reaches of the Roman Empire, the city Lutetia, as the Romans called it, was a mere outpost until Julian built a palace for himself in AD358. Barbarians, Parisii boatmen, and Romans fought frequently on the surrounding plain and all left their mark on the developing character of the Parisians.

Attila the Hun was an unwelcome visitor in the 5th century. The legend of St Geneviève, the patron saint of Paris, was created when she 'saved' the city from his horde. A mere 19-year-old, she assured the citizens that the Huns would spare the city, and when her forecast proved correct, a cult formed around her.

Clovis I brought his Frankish armies to Gaul shortly thereafter, defeating the Gallo-Romans at Soissons. He consolidated his power by beating the Alemanni tribe at Tolbiac in 496 and the Visigoths near Poitiers in 507. Clovis moved the capital to Paris and the Merovingian dynasty was underway. He built the Church of the Apostles to honour the remains of St Geneviève

Clovis I

Culture

City Symbol

and was buried there himself. Now the Panthéon sits on the hill, the final resting place for distinguished citizens such as Victor Hugo and Rousseau.

The Capetian dynasty, which began in 987 with Hugues Capet and finally fizzled out 806 years later with the execution of Louis XVI, ruled during a period of growth. The city was improved with public fountains, paved streets, and armed police to maintain order. Paris was emerging as a major European city. All over the country religious fervour inspired the building of some of France's most famous monuments such as Normandy's Mont-St-Michel.

Trade continued to boom throughout the 12th century. Merchants united in powerful guilds, controlling city finance and administration. King Philippe Auguste built a big covered market (Les Halles), improved the waterfront for trade and erected a great wall around the city, protecting it and giving it an urban identity.

The Church remained strong during the difficult Dark Ages and with prosperity grew stronger. In addition to Notre Dame, smaller churches arose in its Gothic likeness, and old Romanesque edifices were restored and rebuilt.

Already a commercial and ecclesiastical centre, Paris also became the centre of scholarship in medieval Europe, and was the first of the great capitals to have a university. A meeting place for scholars and theologians, controversy and debate became part of the city's character, and remain so today.

The upstart scholar Pierre Abelard was the first to attract students to the Left Bank, where the universities of Paris and of the Sorbonne would open (the latter named after Robert de Sorbon). Latin, used in lectures and debates, gave the neighbourhood the name it now bears, *Le Quartier Latin*, still today the city's student centre. The unfortunate Abelard, however, took attracting students too far, and was castrated and sent to a monastery for showing rather too much affection for one, Héloïse.

A City Shaped

In the 14th century, local clothmaker Etienne Marcel led a revolt against the Valois regent, forming an alliance with English forces which in the end led to his losing the support of the majority of his followers. He was assassinated shortly afterwards. All through the Hundred Years' War, control of Paris bounced back and forth between English and French forces. When Joan of Arc laid siege to the city in 1429, Parisians sided with the occupying English and put up stiff resistance. Things finally settled down once Joan of Arc had succeeded in putting Charles VII on the throne.

Joan of Arc

The period of artistic rebirth that followed under François I continued until a religious crisis provoked the St Bartholomew Massacre, in which thousands of Protestants were killed. However, Henri, king of the southwestern realm of Navarre, escaped and became Henri IV. He went on to be one of France's most celebrated kings.

Henri is known to have switched his religion from Catholic to Protestant and back at least six times, with apparently no qualms at all. The most memorable occasion was upon his triumphant conquest of Paris. He chose that moment to convert to Catholicism, in order to please the powerful Church fathers of Paris as well as the general population. 'Paris,' he said, 'is well worth a mass.'

Thus began the Bourbon monarchy, France's last. The family lavished plenty of money on the city of Paris, trying to keep the unpredictable citizens, the powerful guilds and the Church content. Louis XIV built hospitals and factories, paved new streets and equipped the city with lanterns. Nonetheless, he preferred to move

to his luxurious palace at Versailles, where he was in less danger than in the gloomy old Louvre, surrounded as it was by narrow alleys crowded with houses right up to the palace walls. That was altogether too close to the common people.

The new court was moved wholesale out to Versailles, where the splendour of the architecture and the rigidity of court etiquette imposed by Louis reduced the nobility to mere courtiers whose most important responsibility might be to hand the king his undershirt at the *Levée du Roi* ('kingrise' as opposed to sunrise). Five hundred cooks prepared Louis' food, and he commanded 4,000 servants.

In the period leading towards the French Revolution, life in Paris took on two distinct forms. On the one hand, wealthy aristocrats and the burgeoning *bourgeoisie* enjoyed sumptuous decadence, carried on intricate social ceremonies and whirled through the restaurants and theatres of Paris. On the bleaker side, most of the population lived in growing misery, while government debts piled up and up. A bad harvest in 1788 increased the price of bread and revolution fermented as a result.

The storming of the Bastille prison, on 14 July 1789, has long been the symbol of the violent Revolution that shook all of France. As it was the centre of Revolutionary activities and government, as well as the showcase for the notorious guillotine, Paris was, after the Revolution, unassailably confirmed as the capital of power. 'Paris goes her own way,' wrote Victor Hugo, 'and France, irritated, is forced to follow.' In fact it has been said several times since that Paris has almost become a mini-state in its own right, a massive urban area in an essentially rural country.

The Making of Modern Paris

Through the First Empire, the Restoration, and the Second Republic, Paris continued to solidify its position as the centre of government, arts, fashion and trade, and was regarded as one of Europe's finest capi-

The Coronation of Napoleon Bonaparte

tals, despite its sordid slums and the fundamentally squalid living conditions of the lower classes.

Under the Second Empire (1852–1870) Paris underwent the transformation into the modern city of today. Napoleon III (nephew of Bonaparte) worked with Baron Haussmann, the Prefect of Paris, to carry out extensive urban renewal. Train tracks were set out in all directions, water mains and a sewerage system were installed, great boulevards and avenues were systematically laid out. Slums were razed and the poorest of the poor were displaced outside the city into the eastern suburbs.

The last great struggle between the Parisian population and the wealthy *bourgeoisie* took place after the fall of the Empire under the Third Republic. Hostile to the notion of Prussian occupation following the defeat of Napoleon Bonaparte's army and the Republic's capitulation, the citizens withstood a long siege. When the popular National Guard was ordered to disarm, the *Commune de Paris* was proclaimed at the Hôtel de Ville (town hall).

From the Montmartre hilltop came the call to arms, as workers and revolutionaries united in the struggle for better representation in government. The bloody repression was carried out not by the Prussians, but by regular French troops: 25,000 *communards* died fighting or were executed. This bitter and tragic ending is still a sore spot in the Parisian heart, especially in Montmartre, home to many of the revolutionaries and anarchists who led the battle. Many of the traditional songs heard in cabarets there still recall the *Commune de Paris*.

Providing good service

Paris in the 20th Century

The turn of the century is often referred to as *La Belle Epoque*, a period of gaiety and artistic renewal. The Eiffel Tower rose unbelievably high over the city and the Metro tunnelled below. Between 1880 and 1940, Paris was home to more artists, writers and musicians than any other city in the world, both foreign and French, including Picasso, Debussy, Zola, ballet dancer and impresario Diaghilev, and the singer Edith Piaf.

In World War I the city was saved heroically when General Gallieni rushed troops to a counter-offensive in the Marne River valley using all available means. Every taxi in town was requisitioned to carry soldiers to the front.

During World War II, Paris was not so lucky, and suffered German occupation for four long and dreary years. The city was not

Celebrating the liberation of Paris at the end of World War II

destroyed, however, although charges of dynamite had been placed strategically under monuments. In fact, the German Commander Von Cholitz had orders to blow the city up if the Allies arrived, but he wisely chose to surrender instead. Under General de Gaulle's leadership, the Resistance grew steadily throughout the war, and the troops of the Free French were instrumental in the North African and other campaigns.

Less memorable in retrospect was the role played by the autonomous region of Vichy France, led by World War I general Marshal Pétain. Collaboration with the Nazis was the policy in this region, even though that policy had harrowing implications for the city's Jewish population in particular. In the end, 25 August 1944 was one of the craziest and happiest days in the city's history, partly because General Eisenhower diplomatically allowed the French troops, under the leadership of General Leclerc, to be the first to enter Paris.

After the rationing, death and horrors of war, Paris prospered in the 1950s and early 60s. Bebop, Rock and Roll and tourists travelled across the Atlantic. In May 1968, the city saw its most important upheaval since the Commune. Opponents to the Algerian War, disenchanted students and trade unions struck together and paralysed Paris. Charles de Gaulle himself fled the city, just as kings and emperors had done before him, fearful of the wrath of its

De Gaulle became unpopular

citizens. He relinquished power to his former prime minister Georges Pompidou.

In 1977, reform made it possible for Parisians to elect a mayor for the first time. Jacques Chirac was the first to enjoy this powerful position. In addition, each *arrondissement* elects its own mayor, and the administration of many city affairs is delegated out to separate town halls. In 1989 France celebrated the bicentennial of the French Revolution, an event which led to an orgy of self-congratulation, and major celebrations in Paris. The Eiffel Tower in particular had a complete overhaul.

In 1995 the then Mayor of Paris, Jacques Chirac, was elected as the fifth President of France, ousting François Mitterrand, who had held office for 14 years. Like Napoleon III, Mitterrand left behind a legacy of public works in the city: radical improvements at the Louvre Museum, including the Pyramid by IM Pei enclosing its main entrance, the Opéra at La Bastille, the new Finance Ministry at Bercy, the Grande Arche at La Défense, the La Villette Museum and Science Park, the Arab World Institute opposite the Ile St Louis, the Orsay Museum, many extensive new road and tunnel systems to ease traffic, the development of outlying areas, and improved public transport.

Tour de Paris

The result of all these new projects, combined with the 19th-century achievements of Philippe Auguste and Baron Haussmann, is a striking yet harmonious cityscape.

The spirit of the city today is still a mixture of fractious Gaulish rebellion and refined Roman arts, spiced with the exotic contributions of immigrants from Africa and Asia. A mad poet in Montmartre, a fashion model in diamonds at the Dior boutique, an African student on the Left Bank, an early-rising baker kneading *croissants*: Paris is home to all. Its streets are living theatres, so walk them and observe.

Historical Highlights

52BC: *Lutetia* founded by the Romans and occupied by the Parisii.

AD300: Germanic invasions by the Alemanni tribe. The city settles on the Ile de la Cité and takes the name of Paris.

451: Paris repels the Huns with the help of St Geneviève, who becomes the focal point of a cult.

6th century: The Frankish people settle in Paris.

987: The Capetian dynasty begins, bringing years of prosperity.

12th century: Trade booms. The cathedral of Notre Dame is built on the Ile de la Cité. Philippe Auguste orders the construction of a great wall around the city.

13th century: The Universities of Paris and the Sorbonne created.

1356–8: Revolt led by cloth-maker Etienne Marcel against the Valois dynasty. Marcel was assassinated after making an alliance with the hated English.

1572: Fervent religious debate leads to the St Bartholomew massacre, in which thousands of Protestants died.

1594: Henri IV takes Paris.

1682: Louis XIV moves into Versailles palace and turns the nobility into mere courtiers.

1789: The storming and capture of the Bastille prison heralds the French Revolution.

1793: Execution of Louis XVI.

1804–48: The first Empire, under Napoleon Bonaparte is declared, and is then followed by the Restoration of the (constitutional) Monarchy.

1848: Revolution in Paris, the Second Republic is declared.

1860: The number of *arrondissements*, or districts, rises from only 12 to 20. Today's smart 16th has its designation changed from the unlucky 13th.

1853–70: Under the Second Empire and Napoleon III, nephew of Bonaparte, Baron Haussmann gives Paris its present shape and appearance, particularly notable for its grand boulevards.

1870–1: Paris is under siege by the Prussian Army.

1871: The *Commune de Paris* civil rebellion ends in bloodshed. Many of the rebels are executed in the Père Lachaise cemetery.

1889: The World Fair provokes the construction of several key monuments, most notably the Eiffel Tower.

1940–4: The German army occupies Paris. Liberation comes on 25 August 1944.

1968: General strike (led by the student population) paralyses the city. General de Gaulle, now very unpopular, eventually hands over power to Georges Pompidou.

1977: Death of Pompidou.

1977: Elections for mayor are held for the first time, Jacques Chirac becomes the first incumbent of the Hôtel de Ville (town hall).

1981: François Mitterrand, President of the Republic, initiates a major plan for renewing the city including Le Grand Louvre, the Opéra at the Bastille, the Grande Arche of La Défense, etc.

1989: Celebrations in honour of the Bicentennial of the French Revolution, and 100th birthday of the Eiffel Tower.

1995: In May erstwhile mayor of Paris Jacques Chirac is elected president of France. In November and December the city is paralysed by striking public sector workers.

1996: The death of François Mitterrand.

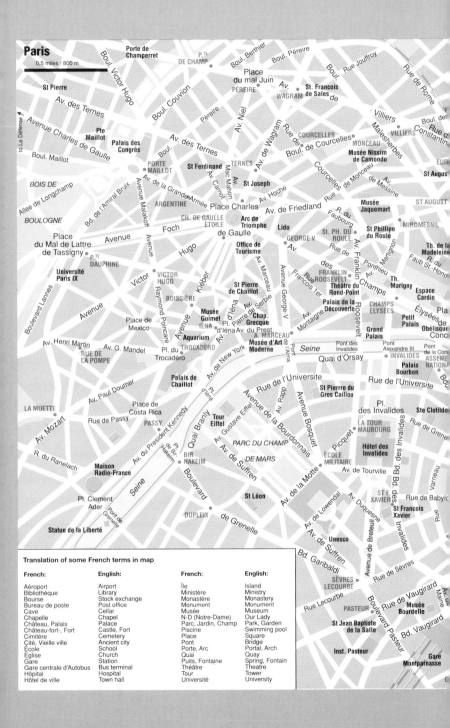

Paris

0,5 miles / 800 m

to La Défense

Translation of some French terms in map

French:	English:	French:	English:
Aéroport	Airport	Île	Island
Bibliothèque	Library	Ministère	Ministry
Bourse	Stock exchange	Monastère	Monastery
Bureau de poste	Post office	Monument	Monument
Cave	Cellar	Musée	Museum
Chapelle	Chapel	N-D (Notre-Dame)	Our Lady
Château, Palais	Palace	Parc, Jardin, Champ	Park, Garden
Château-fort-, Fort	Castle, Fort	Piscine	Swimming pool
Cimitère	Cemetery	Place	Square
Cité, Vieille ville	Ancient city	Pont	Bridge
École	School	Porte, Arc	Portal, Arch
Église	Church	Quai	Quay
Gare	Station	Puits, Fontaine	Spring, Fountain
Gare centrale d'Autobus	Bus terminal	Théâtre	Theatre
Hôpital	Hospital	Tour	Tower
Hôtel de ville	Town hall	Université	University

Day itineraries

DAY ①

Notre Dame and the Left Bank

Begin this full day in Paris where the city itself first started, Ile de la Cité, on an island in the middle of the river Seine. Visit the Gothic cathedral of Notre Dame. From there, wind through the mosaic of streets on the Left (south) Bank. Discover the Latin Quarter, a student hang-out since Roman times, with its mix of scholarship and entertainment. To the Luxembourg Gardens, the park most loved by Parisians, and from there to the city's tallest office building, La Tour Montparnasse, in time for sunset.

Begin early in the morning and wear your most comfortable footwear. This walking tour takes you from the centre of the city towards

Sainte Chapelle, within the Conciergerie

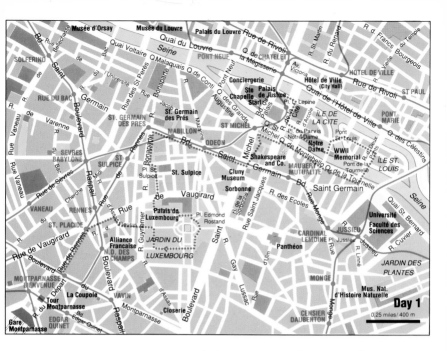

its southern end, with plenty of places to stop and rest your feet on the way. So travel at your leisure; you can always hop on the Metro to speed to the next destination, particularly towards the end of the day.

On the **Ile de la Cité** (Metro: Cité), one of two islands in the Seine, site of the earliest primitive city and later the Roman administrative centre, is the main office of the French police and the Court of Justice, all in the grand **Conciergerie**. This imposing château stands on the foundations of the city's first royal dwelling. Later it held prisoners during the French Revolution, including Queen Marie Antoinette.

In this pompous setting is a diamond, the **Sainte Chapelle**, with a tall and sharp silhouette which is clearly visible in the overall complex. This narrow and vaulted Gothic chapel (follow the sign inside the main entrance on the Cour du Mai) was built by Saint Louis, King of France, in 1264. The deep-coloured glass windows set in scalloped stonework and the excellent restoration of the walls and columns lend the building a delicate beauty. Fans of chamber music may wish to note the bulletin board detailing concert schedules. The chapel is open daily except on public holidays, from 9.30 am–6pm, but is occasionally inaccessible when high-profile trials occupy the court-rooms next door.

The Conciergerie

Turn back towards Notre Dame via the pedestrian **Place Lepine**, for the daily flower and bird market. Flower sellers are here from 9am–7pm except Sunday, when song-birds are the speciality.

Now walk round the corner to

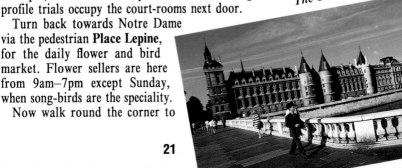

21

Gargoyle on Notre Dame

the **Parvis de Notre Dame**, a cobbled square in front of the great cathedral (open daily 8am–7pm; tours available). **Notre Dame**'s stone foundation was laid in 1163 but it was only completed about 200 years later. The scene of various dramatic episodes in French history, from medieval executions to the coronation of an Emperor (Napoleon I), the cathedral's ancient walls are steeped in history, reflected in the innumerable faces and figures carved upon them. The three portals (main doorways) to the cathedral are typical examples of Gothic religious art, each a 'book' for the illiterate of the Middle Ages, recounting the stories of the Bible and the lives of various saints. Inside, 29 separate chapels line the nave, transept and choir. The **Rose Windows**, 31ft (9 metres) in diameter, have been extensively restored but parts of them still date from the 13th century.

The carved wooden choir stalls are early 17th century, and the **Pietà Statue** decorating the large altar at the far end of the cathedral was commissioned by Louis XIII during the same period, an offering in thanks for the birth of his son and heir to the throne, who eventually completed the memorial. In veneration on either side of the fallen Christ and his earthly mother are statues of the regal father and son.

The **Treasury** (Trésor) (closed on Sunday and religious holidays), off the south aisle to the right of the High Altar, is the cathedral's treasury, displaying religious artifacts, embroidered robes and jewelled chalices. The **Crypt** (open daily 10am–5.30pm; entrance charge) focuses on Paris's archaeological finds from the Roman period until the 19th century.

As you leave the church, you will see signs to the **Bell Tower**, and if you are up to a 270-ft (82-metre) spiralling ascent, you can visit the huge brass bell and come eye-to-eye with the gargoyles who contemplate the city from their privileged perch.

Leave the cathedral, walk around it to the right, go through the little park and to the end of the island. There you will find an unusual and starkly moving monument in memory of World War II deportees to German concentration camps (**Mémorial des Martyrs de la Déportation**, open daily; closed noon–2pm) set down into the ground. Descend into the pit through narrow passages between thick, rough walls, and come face to

Maison Berthillon, famous for ice cream

face with black metal bars. There is a feeling of desolation, yet the monument is strangely calm: a windless sun-trap inviting rest and reflection.

From there, take the Pont St Louis to the next island, the placid **Ile St Louis**. The attractions of this 'island of calm' in the storm of the city are the shady riverfront, the fashionable art galleries, cosy, lace-curtained tea rooms (try **La Charlotte de l'Ile** for the ultimate hot chocolate and Wednesday afternoon puppet shows). At 31 Rue St Louis en l'Ile (the other end of the bridge from Ile de la Cité) is **Maison Berthillon**, where you can sample possibly the best ice-cream in Paris while sitting in the sun.

Afterwards backtrack across Ile de la Cité and cross the Seine to the Left Bank, where a walk along the *quai* affords a fine view of Notre Dame and its flying buttresses, as well as an opportunity to browse among the characteristic green bookstalls, which also sell unusual postcards, prints and maps. There are some collector's items to be ferreted out here.

More books, new and second-hand in English mostly, are in store

Notre Dame seen from the south

at the historic **Shakespeare and Co.** in Rue de la Bûcherie, just off the left of the tiny Square Viviani (Metro: St Michel or Cluny Sorbonne). The spirit of famous (and would-be famous) expatriate writers haunts the shop, which is well worth exploring.

Head south into the narrow lanes and the centre of the **Latin Quarter**, one of the busiest parts of town and favoured by students, shoppers and good-time seekers. These narrow ways, filled in the evening with the aromas of Greek and Middle Eastern cooking and busy with strolling entertainers, recall much older times, despite the electric lights and modern fashions. Street performers set up here as they have for centuries, and pass a hat among the crowd. Through the occasional kitchen door left ajar you may see a chef spooning up steaming heaps of Algerian *couscous*. But although this is a popular tourist quarter for good-value dining out, where restaurateurs blatantly entice pasersby in to sample their fare, you shouldn't expect to find the best cuisine in Paris.

Books on the Boulevard St Michel

At the minuscule **Théâtre de la Huchette**, the troupe has been playing *The Bald Soprano* for over 50 years. Tickets are available. Amble down the pedestrian streets of La Huchette and La Harpe up to **Boulevard St Michel**. Walk up to the crossroads with **Boulevard St Germain**, where the two big roads meet and thereby set the limits of the famous Latin Quarter.

On the far corner stands the **Musée National du Moyen-Age – Thermes de Cluny** (9.15am–5.45pm, closed Tuesday and public holidays), the city's only surviving Gothic residence, next to the ruins of a Roman bath house, a 2nd-century vestige. This is really one of the best museums in a city which boasts some of the world's finest. The building lends itself perfectly to the display of furnishings, fabrics, stained glass, architectural ornaments and religious reliquaries from the Middle Ages. Upstairs, the museum's prize is the tapestry series *La Dame à la Licorne* (*The Lady and the Unicorn*), a 15th-century depiction of the five senses plus a sixth, mysterious and unexplained sense that is left to your imagination.

After much medieval food for thought, you may be hungry. You will find plenty

In the Musée National

A legend in St Germain des Prés

of choice for lunch up the Blvd St Germain at the crossroads called **Odéon** (Metro: Odéon). I recommend the **Chope d'Alsace**, 4 Carrefour de l'Odéon (tel: 01 43266776), which will satisfy the heartiest appetite with typical food from Eastern France (especially *choucroute* – sauerkraut with pork cuts and sausages), grilled meat and seafood. The list of daily specials, often as long as the regular menu, is based on the chef's mood and the morning's market. Prices are fair for the quality and quantity served, and the wine list is tempting.

Thus revived, your next step is to continue up Boulevard St Michel towards **St Germain des Prés**. Along the way, you pass Rue de Buci on the right-hand side and Rue Mabillon on the left, both leading to colourful markets. There are boutiques for every kind of clothes all along the way, from the classic Marcel Fuks for men to the wacky, unisex Atomic City and shops for parents of fashion-conscious children (or vice versa).

The church of **St Germain des Prés** (Metro: St Germain des Prés), is one of the city's oldest (built in the 11th and 12th centuries, Romanesque in style). The square is also well known for the cafés **Flore** (tel: 01 45485526) and **Les Deux Magots** and the **Brasserie Lipp** (tel: 01 45485391), hangouts for the literati since Jean-Paul Sartre and Simone de Beauvoir held court here.

Turn down Rue Bonaparte, away from the church and towards Montparnasse, to find more stylish shops on and around the pleasant **Place Saint Sulpice** (Metro: St Sulpice). Less animated than St

St Sulpice, where Victor Hugo married

Germain, this square and its 18th-century fountain have a dignified charm.

The church, where author Victor Hugo was married, is welcoming despite its monumental proportions; there is a fine old pipe organ inside (check the bulletin board for the schedule of concerts); the first chapel on the right (Chapelle de Sainte Agnès) was decorated by Eugène Delacroix, one of the greatest painters of the Romantic period. As you leave St Sulpice, look up to the building on the other side of the square. This is where many Parisians would spare a glance, hoping to catch a glimpse of France's favourite actress Catherine Deneuve leaning out of her window.

As afternoon wends its way to evening, just a short walk down Rue Henry de Jouvenel (immediately left out of the church) and Rue Ferou brings you to the **Jardin du Luxembourg**. Enter by the **Petit Luxembourg Museum**, which has changing exhibitions, and reach the central pond by way of the **Palais du Luxembourg**, once a royal palace and today the seat of the French Senate. If you stroll to the far end of the gardens and look over the top of the palace, you should be able to see Sacré Coeur perched on the Montmartre hilltop, like a fat white pigeon roosting above the city.

Take a break in the sunshine under the shade of the chestnut trees. The Jardin du Luxembourg is much more of a recreation area than the Tuileries, and a particular favourite with many Parisians because of its elegance and its central location. But don't linger here after dark, or you'll find yourself camping out for the night

Parisians enjoy the Jardin du Luxembourg

behind high locked gates, which are closed at nightfall by bell-ringing guardians.

Leave the park by the west exit (level with the round pond) onto Rue de Fleurus, where Gertrude Stein and her life-long companion Alice B Toklas lived and reigned over artistic society and the 'Lost Generation' at No 27. Their *coterie* included Hemingway, Picasso, Ford Madox Ford, Cézanne, Matisse and other artists in the period from 1907 to Stein's death in 1946.

Continue some way down Fleurus before turning right on Notre Dame des Champs (Metro: St Placide) to reach Rue de Rennes. From there you can walk straight down to Montparnasse (or take the Metro) to arrive at the **Tour Montparnasse** at its southern end.

To get a superb view over the territory you've covered, take the superfast elevator (9.30am–10.30pm, until 11.30pm in summer; admission fee; last lift 30 minutes before closing time) to the 56th-floor terrace and rooftop of the tower. At this height, the traffic below is seen but not heard; and wide avenues ribboned in green trees stretch away below the rooftops with their characteristic red chimney pots. The glassed-in bar provides signs with information on what you are seeing from each point of reference. But the helicopter pad on the very top (59 floors up) is more exciting; open to the wind and seemingly unbounded on the sides, it feels a little dangerous (there is no real danger, in fact) – which may be why there are not usually many people up here. To see where you've been during the day, look due north and you should spot the green sward of the Luxembourg gardens, and a little further in the distance, the two solid square towers of Notre Dame.

For dinner

At dusk, the sun sets beyond the Eiffel Tower. On a good clear evening, Montparnasse is the ideal place to watch the natural fireworks at the end of day, and the sparkles of artificial light blooming across the city landscape.

Back on the street, you can head for dinner at one of Hemingway's favourite haunts: **La Closerie des Lilas** (171 Blvd Montparnasse, tel: 01 40513450) or **La Coupole** (102 on the same street, tel: 01 43201420). The first is rather special; it has a laid-back atmosphere and a piano bar and is more expensive as well as being some way down the boulevard. The second is a large and noisy place to dance, eat, see and be seen. Both have varied menus; for a complete meal with wine, count on at least 200 Francs per person. They're open late, as are many of the local cafés and bars, and there are plenty of taxis to take you back to your hotel.

The Grand Boulevards

Today's itinerary begins with a panoramic view of Paris from the Arc de Triomphe. This is the Paris of the grand and sweeping avenues, created by Baron Haussmann in the mid-19th century. Start by walking down the Champs Elysées to Place de la Concorde and the Tuileries; side-step the Louvre to the Palais Royal and on to the redeveloped Halles and the Georges Pompidou Centre.

The first half of this day is spent walking the long straight line known as the **Triumphal Way**. A major feature of Paris, it is not very intimate, and perhaps no longer the most spectacular, even though it has been extended right out to the new Grande Arche at La Défense. The Champs Elysées is still the most famous part of this route. (A hint for those with tired feet: ride down the avenue in green bus No 73 and save some energy for later).

Up the Champs Elysées

A familiar landmark, the grand **Arc de Triomphe** (Metro: Charles de Gaulle-Etoile) straddles a hectic cobbled traffic circle. Construction began in 1806, but it wasn't completed until 30 years later, all in commemoration of the victories of Napoleon Bonaparte. In 1920, the arch became the site for the **Tomb of the Unknown Soldier**; a Flame of Remembrance was lit.

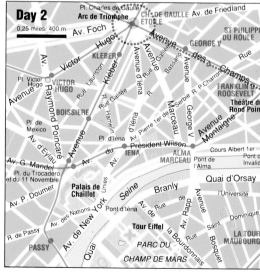

28

Tomb of the Unknown Soldier

It was the 'other' Napoleon (nephew of the Corsican original, known to some as 'Napoleon the Little') who ordered the city planning that gave the **Place de l'Etoile** ('of the star') its name. With the Prefect of Paris, Baron Haussmann, he created the city's wide boulevards flanked by chestnut trees, including the 12 avenues that radiate out from the Arc de Triomphe. Partly motivated by the need to control rebellious crowds (hence the wide, straight thoroughfares), the two of them created an architectural legend, and greatly advanced the art of urban planning.

You can take an elevator to the top of the Arc de Triomphe (10am–10.30pm; closes 6pm Sunday and Monday, 6.30pm in summer). The view is still largely the same as it was when Haussmann had finished with the city, and includes the spacious **Bois de Boulogne** forest to the west and, of course, the **Avenue des Champs Elysées** at your feet.

One hundred years ago, this glitzy strip was little more than a bridlepath, suitable for closed carriage rides and intimate suppers in discreet restaurants. Luxurious private homes later gave way to sumptuous hotels, expensive shops and desirable corporate addresses. Now, the avenue sparkles at night – not with the diamonds and bright personalities of its heyday but with heavy traffic and neon lights.

Cinemas, cafés and fast food places provide most of the

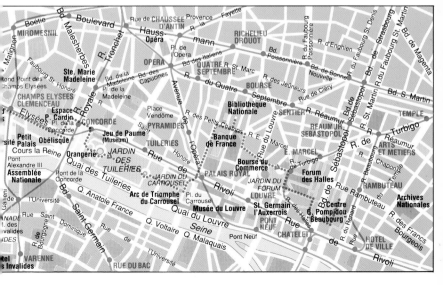

entertainment today; the shops and restaurants are generally overpriced and aimed at tourists; and the people walking up and down the avenue are mostly foreigners or teenagers from the suburbs who come in for hamburgers and a film.

Despite the fading reputation, it is still fun to stroll down the wide pavements of the Champs Elysées and people watch. The top end is dominated by airline offices and the **Tourist Office**, on the south side. On the same side half way down is the **Hotel George V** (on the avenue of the same name, Metro: George V), which is beautifully decorated with a fine restaurant and garden terrace.

The size of the Champs Elysées is emphasised by stores such as the **Hippo Citroen** or the **Pub Renault**, where you can check out the latest car models and the Renault Museum over a thick steak or a beer, and the **Virgin Megastore**, a truly mega book and record shop. At the bottom of the slope, where the avenue opens out, you will find **Le Drugstore** (tel: 01 44437900), which has outlived its fashionableness, but still draws a crowd to its American-style restaurant.

Hotel George V

At this point the avenue becomes far more attractive in summer, with its serene fountains and shady park, with several interesting theatres. To the right just down Avenue Franklin Roosevelt is the **Rond Point (Théâtre Renaud-Barrault)**, which was created by two of France's finest actors, who also happen to be living one of the longest-running love stories ever. You can walk in for a look at the fun décor, or stop for a drink in the bar. The restaurant **Laserre** (tel: 01 43595343) is a little further down this avenue on the right, opposite the Palais de la Découverte. This discreet building is one of the top 10 restaurants in town – for both cuisine and price! Count on at least 500 Francs per person, but the choice of wine from the outstanding cellar may make that substantially higher.

Back in the parkland on the left of the Champs Elysées, the **Espace Pierre Cardin** (half-way to Place de la Concorde) is another prestigious performance space, where a garden restaurant (a favourite with celebrities) features a buffet lunch.

The **Place de la Concorde**, and its commanding, 33-centuries-old obelisk from the tomb of Ramses III in Egypt, is another city landmark. Eighty-five thousand square yards (70,833sq m) of cobblestone, the Place is known for its fast and furious traffic. It was here, in January 1793, that Louis XVI was beheaded. His last words were: 'May my blood bring happiness to France.'

Fountain, Place de la Concorde

Dash across the traffic into the relative peace of the **Jardin des Tuileries**, the long narrow gardens leading to the Louvre. The central alley is part of the long straight line from the Arc de Triomphe. Haussmann left his mark here, too, tearing down the remains of a castle and opening up the streets. The sunny pools and patches of green lawn alternate with shaded alleys where you'll find outdoor cafés, a children's play area, and finally, almost inside the encircling arms of the Palais du Louvre, the **Arc de Triomphe du Carrousel**, a miniature mirror-image of the Arc de Triomphe which marks the end of the lengthy Triumphal Way. The gardens have been having a facelift which should be completed by the end of 1998 as part of the New Louvre project.

At this stage, if the Louvre beckons, turn to itinerary 6: *The New Louvre*, page 69. But I suggest you postpone the Louvre visit, and leave the Tuileries behind to dive across the busy **Rue de Rivoli**. Walk through the arcades past the gilded statue of Joan of Arc to the Place du Palais Royal (Metro: Palais Royal). The adjacent Place Colette is home to the **Comédie Française**, the famous classical theatre founded by Molière. Follow the arcades to the entrance of the **Palais Royal Gardens**. About 200 years ago, the Palais really was a royal palace, until Philippe d'Orléans, who was living there, sank deep into debt. He added arcades and rented boutique space to solve his cash-flow problem. It became a very popular speakers' corner and played an important role in the Revolution.

Today the shops are still there, beyond the square of black and white columns designed by Burennes, which are matched by the window shades of the surrounding buildings. Most of the shops offer antiques and collector's items, especially coins and military decorations. These dim little boutiques are full of uncommon treasures for those who know how to value them.

Between the Champs Elysées and the Tuileries

Galerie Colbert

Part of the Palais is now occupied by the Ministry of Culture; other apartments are still in private hands. It is said that these apartments are beyond price – families hang on to them forever. It is easy to see why: they are centrally located yet quiet, soothing to the eye and spirit. Sometimes you can glimpse a high-ceilinged room behind a heavy brocade curtain. Even the children running through the park have something of another era about them, as they play ageless games among the sandy paths.

Slip out the far end of the rectangular gardens and cross the tiny Rue des Petits Champs. To your left are the **Galerie Vivienne** and the **Galerie Colbert**, recently restored skylit passages with mosaic walkways, leading to Rue Vivienne and the old French National Library, not far from the Opéra. To your right is the **Place des Victoires**, a charming circle which was originally built to display the statue of Louis XIV in the centre. Now fashion is king both in the Place and the narrow streets radiating out from it. The designers' boutiques are New Age outposts in the regal architecture.

Around the corner (past the main post office on Rue du Louvre) is the restaurant **Au Pied de Cochon** (tel: 01 40137700), one of the best-known in Paris, in a row of restaurants on Rue Coquillière. As a carry-over from older times, when market deliveries were made in the wee hours before stalls opened up, it is open day and night. One of the favourite dishes of the hard-working market hands was the thick and cheesy onion soup, still on the menu. For a complete meal, you should count on 250 Francs per person.

You are now on the fringes of **Les Halles**, visible here as a covered-in parkland with escalators down to the shopping centre. The name refers to the city food market which clogged up the neighbourhood streets

Les Halles and St Eustache

from the 12th century until 1969, when it was demolished in the interests of safety and urban renewal. Now a more ordinary commerce takes place in about 200 boutiques of every sort inside the multi-level shopping centre (Metro: Les Halles).

But don't go down the escalators – unless you really want to go shopping. Instead, have a quick look inside the rather sombre and grand **St Eustache** to your left. Then take a walk around the edge of the parkland by way of Rue Berger to the lively **Place des Innocents**, where there's usually a good crowd gathered around the fountain. The square is the setting for a permanent fashion parade. Parisians who knew it before renewal deplore the high-priced boutiques and cafés that have moved in, but it is as animated and attractive as ever.

At the corner of Rue Berger and **Rue St Denis**, take a good look up and down. Rue St Denis marks the beginning of the city's main red-light area, which gets more overt several blocks further down to the left. The area in which you stand is fairly tame, and although there are plenty of sex shops there are also lots of cheap eateries and interesting shops. One of the nicest places is **The Front Page**, offering American specialities like spare ribs and chilli and an American-style bar.

All the comings and goings in the pedestrian areas, the variety of commerce and nightlife help Les Halles retain something of its former dynamism from the days when it was the city's main market. Drifters, bargain hunters, sensation seekers, local residents and young people mix like a crazy salad. Hang on to your wallet.

Head south from Place des Innocents towards the river and then turn left onto Rue des Lombards. Use it to cross Boulevard Sebastopol into the region of Paris known as the Marais. Instantly you will find yourself in the Marais' characteristic narrow, winding streets with small shops and bars. Turn left up Rue St Martin to **St Merri**, an ornate medieval church nestled tightly amidst the shops and restaurants. You may hear music floating out of its doors, for there are frequent concerts in the church, particularly at weekends. The church bell has been tolling the hours since 1331 and is the oldest in Paris.

Now you are just around the corner from the most visited attraction (twice the numbers for the Louvre) in the city, the modern museum, known affection-ately as 'Beaubourg' after the street which runs behind it, has been looming on your horizon ever since Les Halles. Its official name is the **Georges Pompidou Arts and Cultural Centre** (Metro: Rambuteau: Wednesday to Friday noon–10pm; Saturday and Sunday 10am–10pm), and it acts

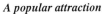

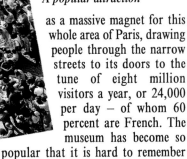

as a massive magnet for this whole area of Paris, drawing people through the narrow streets to its doors to the tune of eight million visitors a year, or 24,000 per day – of whom 60 percent are French. The museum has become so popular that it is hard to remember the passionate debate about its 'inside-out' architecture (blue units are air-conditioning, green are water circulation, red are transport routes and yellow indicates electric circuits). Comments like 'looks like an oil refinery' are rarely heard today. Although the building was beginning to show signs of wear and tear, the entire outside of the building has recently been renvovated, and what goes on inside is still as exciting as ever.

While many Paris museums seem to be staid, whispery places, this one is an exception, even before you enter. Fire-eaters, mimes, musicians and an assorted crew of urban nomads have adopted the sloping cobbled terrace. Students love the library and music room. The ride is free on the escalators that snake up the outside of the building in a transparent tube to the fifth-floor rooftop cafeteria and viewing platform. By the south end of the building is a quartz clock counting the seconds to the year 2000. And further south, between Beaubourg and the St Merri church, is a colourful fountain of grotesque creatures mixed with modern inventions spouting water in different directions. It is much appreciated by children.

The Pompidou's permanent collection is the **National Museum of Modern Art**, on the fourth floor. There is a more serious art-appreciation atmosphere in these well-lit and comfortable rooms. Paintings and sculptures include works from different periods and schools: Fauvism, Cubism, Futurism and various artists including Matisse, Kandinsky, Mondrian and Dubuffet. These permanent exhibitions are well worth the visit, and generally not too crowded. If you find yourself faced by a long queue, it is probably for a temporary show. Occasionally, they are quite controversial, and you may hear art lovers arguing on the way out.

In the entrance hall, there is generally a free exhibition, invariably something zany and challenging. It could be, for example, a show of household lamp

design, some sample 'sonic environments' to immerse oneself in, or an exhibition of mud and clay architecture. On the mezzanine level is a post office and an internet café.

The **Salle Garance** is for zealous cinephiles, specialising in films that don't often make it to local theatres. For avant garde sounds, there is the IRCAM (Institute of Research and Co-ordination into Acoustics and Music), a prestigious centre directed by Pierre Boulez. The museum also welcomes dance and theatre troupes to its basement stage.

There is a complete posting of all the centre's events and exhibits on the ground floor; some things are free. The information booths stock brochures in many languages, and there is a very good bookshop and a gift shop featuring the smaller works of modern designers in the form of pens, household objects, etc.

For dinner this evening, I suggest one of two options. The first, **Restaurant du Palais Royal** (tel: 01 40200027) at 43 rue Valois, is a popular dining spot overlooking the Palais Royal gardens. You can expect to pay around 200 Francs per person.

Spoilt for choice

Alternatively try the rather less chic but just as French 'Smoking Dog', **Au Chien Qui Fume** (tel: 01 42360742), in a quiet corner at the top of Rue du Pont Neuf. Shellfish and hearty French cooking at reasonable prices, as well as all-day service from noon until 2am (costs around 170 Francs per person).

Georges Pompidou Arts and Cultural Centre (Beaubourg)

DAY 3

Marais and Bastille

This itinerary takes you through one of the most distinctive and well-loved areas of Paris: the Marais. The beauty of the buildings lining the narrow, twisted streets can be traced to the 16th and 17th centuries, when well-to-do Parisians built their 'hôtels particuliers' (private residences).

In this itinerary, south of Rue St Antoine is not as interesting as the area north. Therefore, if time is short, go straight from the Hôtel de Ville to St Paul by Metro, then begin at the Hôtel de Sully. The section of the itinerary that goes beyond the Place de Bastille with its shiny new opera house is primarily for those interested in contemporary art and alternative Paris culture. To complete the whole route in a day, choose one or two museums, and content yourself with the windows of most galleries.

You should begin your day at the **Hôtel de Ville** (Metro: Hôtel de Ville). This is the seat of the main branch of local government, and has been the fiefdom of the Mayor of Paris since 1977.

The first Hôtel de Ville was built along the bank of the river Seine during the Renaissance, at the height of the neighbourhood's popularity. It was burned to the ground during the insurrection of the Commune in 1871.

Viollet-le-Duc undertook its reconstruction. This Parisian architect is renowned in France for his restoration and recreation of medieval edifices. Besides the Hôtel de Ville, he restored Notre Dame and other cathedrals, the castle at Pierrefonds, and the entire city of Carcassonne in southwest France.

Hôtel de Ville

There is a convenient post office in the Hôtel de Ville (on the side with the very pleasant courtyard), and on the Rue de Rivoli there is an entrance to an exhibition area with some information about the town.

You may be tempted to tarry on **Rue de Rivoli**. This is a very busy shopping street, with giants like the BHV department store directly opposite, and other speciality shops selling shoes, clothes, pianos, whatever. From here, to your left the street leads right up past the Louvre and to the Place de la Concorde; to your right it leads into Rue St Antoine and the Marais. Most large international chain stores are represented along its length. But to discover the

Restaurant in the Marais

Marais, you must take quieter paths, and I suggest you begin at the **Saint Gervais Church**, which is located in a quiet square on the other (eastern) side of the Hôtel de Ville. The monumental Gothic style of this church is original, not reconstructed. Restoration has been carried out, however, most notably after a German shell exploded here in 1918, killing 51 people at a Good Friday mass.

Continue up Rue François Miron to the left of the church, contemplating the row of houses from No 4 to 14 built in 1732. Farther along, some distance past half-timbered houses on the left, No 68 is another remarkable residence, the **Hôtel de Beauvais**, dating from 1665. Louis XIV gave it to his mistress, and when she was gone, Mozart lived there briefly.

Turn right into Rue du Jouy and go across the crossroads by the Tribunal and into Rue Charlemagne. Hidden away to the right (signposted) in this quiet residential district is the **Bibliothèque Forney**, open in the afternoons. Before it became the city's historical and fine arts library, this building was known as the Hôtel de Sens, which the Archbishop of Sens began building in 1470. The pointed towers on the corners are a familiar landmark to Parisians. Later, the mansion was inhabited by Marguerite de Valois, first wife of Henri IV, notorious for her penchant for young lovers.

Continue down the rather dull Rue Charlemagne to where it suddenly becomes far more interesting at **Rue St Paul** (Metro: St

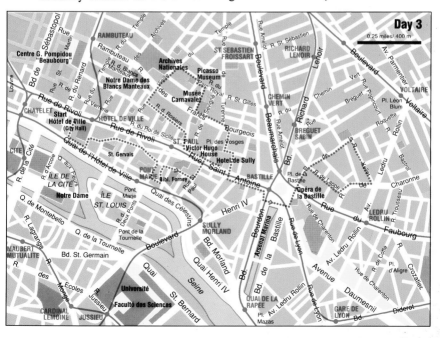

Paul). This little street is a favourite of mine, with its exotic boutiques and restaurants. Take it left up to Rue Saint Antoine. This wide avenue leads back into the Rue de Rivoli, but you should cross it and turn right to reach the **Hôtel de Sully**, which now opens its doors to the public as the *Caisse National des Monuments Historiques*. This umbrella organisation offers the best guided tours of Parisian monuments, museums and sites. Inside, you can visit the lovely courtyard (open for concerts in summer) and the current exhibition, and also pick up an illustrated map of the Marais (weekdays 9am–6pm; Saturday 10am–1.15pm and 2–5pm; closed Sunday and public holidays).

Hôtel de Sully

Retrace your steps down Rue St Antoine past the church, turn right on Rue Malher and go down the **Rue des Rosiers**. This is the heart of the Jewish Quarter, as the specialised shops and restaurants tell you. One of the street's best places to eat is **Jo Goldenberg's** (No 7, tel: 01 42776774). The Goldenbergs came from Russia, and their recipes reflect it. Borscht is a favourite starter here, and stuffed carp is the star of the menu. Prices are moderate, unless you opt for caviar.

Another choice would be to eat your way slowly down the street, stopping at stands for falafel and various sandwiches on pitta or rye bread, pickled lemons, smoked sausages and pastries; sampling a mixture of culinary traditions from both Eastern Europe and the Middle East.

At the end of the street, turn right on Rue Vieille du Temple and follow it up some distance to Rue de la Perle. Turn right again to reach the Place Thorigny and the **Picasso Museum** (1 April to 30 September 9.30am –6pm, 1 October to 31 March 9.30am–5.30pm, closed Tuesday), on the left off a little square. The museum occupies the **Hôtel Salé**, so-called because its 17th-century owner grew rich through the lucrative activity of collecting taxes on salt. Oddly, the very modern masterpieces fit superbly into the well-restored decor. The chandeliers, benches and chairs were designed by Picasso's friend Alberto Giacometti.

The paintings and other works

The Picasso Museum in the Hôtel Salé

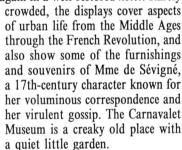

of art were part of the artist's legacy, and are arranged chronologically. There are also a number of works by other artists which were part of his own private collection. The museum opened in 1985, and long queues have been its fate ever since. Nonetheless, it is worth joining them to see so many of this prolific artist's works displayed in one place.

Continue your walk down Rue de Parc Royal, then right into Rue Payenne and past the two pretty little parks bordering it. This part of the Marais has grown more chic since the museum opened, with a number of trendy boutiques and art galleries. Some of them have set up in butcher's or baker's premises, and kept the original shop-fronts. Several other Renaissance *hôtels* are in the midst of restoration.

Stop on the corner of Rue des Francs Bourgeois at **Marais Plus**, a wonderful giftshop and tearoom. The shop has a great collection of the most eccentric teapots (plus a book about them). Refresh yourself with a big piece of freshly baked cake or pie and a pot of fragrant tea.

Just around the corner, a few places to the left on Rue de Sévigné, is the **Carnavalet Museum** (10am–5.40pm, closed Monday). This is the city's historical museum, again in a well-restored *hôtel*. Rarely

crowded, the displays cover aspects of urban life from the Middle Ages through the French Revolution, and also show some of the furnishings and souvenirs of Mme de Sévigné, a 17th-century character known for her voluminous correspondence and her virulent gossip. The Carnavalet Museum is a creaky old place with a quiet little garden.

Walk the rest of the way down the boutique-lined Rue des Francs Bourgeois to the **Place des Vosges**, a highlight of the Marais, and a unique Parisian square. The red brick arcades give it a singular appeal. This is the oldest square in Paris, and its name is in honour of the first French department to pay its taxes to the new Republic.

At the far corner of the square, **Victor Hugo's House** (Maison de Victor Hugo) is open to the public at No 6 (10am–5.40pm, closed

In Place des Vosges

Monday and public holidays). The author of *Les Misérables* was also an expert carpenter: some of the furniture on display was crafted by his own hands.

The covered arcades of the Place des Vosges are animated much as they must have been in Hugo's time, with street singers and accordeon players adding to the atmosphere. Restaurants, tea rooms, fashion boutiques and some interesting shops line the square, and there are shops selling antiques alongside others selling modern items of interior decor for the home. **Coté Hacienda** sells furniture and ceramics from Mexico (another branch on Rue Birague sells tiles). **Max Spira** sells antiques and is good for lighting. One of the prettiest restaurants is **La Guirlande de Julie**.

Leave the Marais down Rue Birague and Rue St Antoine and then turn left for the **Place de la Bastille** (Metro: Bastille). In the centre of the former site of the notorious prison captured on 14 July 1789 stands the **July Column**. It was erected in the last century to honour the victims of the revolutions of 1830 and 1848. Caught in mid-flight high atop is a golden statue, the *Génie de la Bastille*, a representation of Liberty.

The old Bastille prison has long gone. In its stead a new fortress has taken shape, all silver and glass looking very sleek and impenetrable. This is the **Opéra de la Bastille**, one of President François Mitterrand's great projects. Plagued by controversy from the start, and with a multitude of changes in design and administration, the Opéra is now up and running. Time will tell if it achieves its goal of making great music more accessible to the population of Paris.

Your destination now is **Rue de la Roquette**, branching off near the Opéra and heading east all the way to the Père Lachaise cemetery. You are now out of both the winding Marais and the grand and uniform Haussmann's Paris, and away from the tourists. This street is not beautiful, and it becomes increasingly run-down. Once the site of a women's prison where public executions were spectator sports, the street has shed its grisly reputation and is now a trendy place to hang out. If you are ready for dinner, you will find plenty of choice here. There are several Japanese restaurants, and other ethnic styles of cooking are represented.

If eating can wait just wander along the street, which offers an eclectic mix of shops, including a **Model Train Shop**, some small fashion boutiques, and shops specialising in artefacts for the home – they have some very quirky items that might make unusual

July Column, Place de la Bastille

souvenirs. The secondhand bookshop next to the **Théâtre de la Bastille** has a good collection of postcards – not just the usual shots of the Eiffel Tower.

Retrace a few steps, then turn down Rue Keller, where you can visit several small galleries displaying a variety of mainly very modern works. Continue to the end of the street and turn right onto Rue de Charonne where **Lavignes Bastille** is one of the best-known galleries in the neighbourhood. Andy Warhol has exhibited here. The homemade cakes in the window of the **Café Charonne** next door may tempt you in. When refreshed, carry on to the last street on our agenda, the Rue de Lappe, on the right off Charonne. There are more galleries here, with exhibitions that change regularly, so it is impossible to predict exactly what you will find. Prices may be negotiable.

Rue de Lappe is a good place to stop for dinner and enjoy the nightlife. There is a variety of eateries here, offering the cuisine of different countries, including several Spanish tapa bars. One option worth trying is **La Galoche**, at the beginning of the street. The restaurant's name derives from the word for 'shoe' used in the region of Auvergne. Migrants from that province were the first to settle in the neighbourhood, and there are still signs of their influence in the speciality grocer's shops and the faded signs hanging over doorways. La Galoche serves typical hearty fare from the region in a warm friendly atmosphere (expect to pay around 150–200 Francs). You can even buy a pair of wooden shoes here, if you feel especially inspired by the rustic ambience.

Such shoes, however, would not be appropriate footwear for a night of dancing at the **Balajo** (tel: 01 47000787), three-quarters of the way down Rue de Lappe. This fun club is both authentic and inexpensive, with Art Deco flourishes and a big dance

Rue de Lappe delicatessen

floor. The Balajo is just one of several night spots you will find along this street.

If your day's journey has left you feeling tired and unwilling to venture too far for supper, you will be glad to know that you are almost back at the Place de la Bastille, and can head for the **Brasserie Bofinger** (5–7 Rue de la Bastille, just off to the west side of the Place, tel: 01 42728782), one of the city's finest. Settle back and enjoy its comfortable, old-fashioned ambience, brass, mirrors, leather and ceramics. The food is worthy of the oldest brasserie in town. For around 200–250 Francs per person, you can enjoy a real feast; the menu features fresh seafood, *choucroute*, and traditional French dishes and wine.

Bois to Eiffel: Western Paris

Today's itinerary features a part of Paris known by its district number – the 16th – and largely ignored by tourists. It is a luxurious residential area bordering on the spacious western park of Paris, the Bois de Boulogne. Down by the riverside, the district puts on a much more familiar face at Trocadéro, where the monumental and museum-laden Palais de Chaillot opens its two wings to frame the city's most famous landmark: the Eiffel Tower.

This is a long itinerary; you can shorten the walk by starting at the Musée Marmottan, missing the Bois altogether.

On a map, the **Bois de Boulogne** is a large green rectangle bordered on the far western side by a bend in the River Seine and on the inner side by the 16th district of Paris. The main road-entrance to the 2,000-acre (872 ha) park is at **Porte Dauphine** (Metro: Porte Dauphine). Start off early and walk along the Route de Suresne, or venture off the roadway on to the footpaths leading to the **Lac Inférieur**, a long and narrow artificial lake.

In the Bois de Boulogne

You will share your morning stroll with many Parisians. There are always joggers out here, and the lake is popular with rowers. In some parts of the Bois, prostitution is practised rather openly by 'hitchhikers' standing near the roadway. By day this phenomenon is less common.

You may see people waiting for the horses to start running at the **Auteuil Race Track**, studying their racing forms and the sports pages of the daily newspapers. Rose lovers should walk deeper into the park along the Route aux Lacs and the Route de Bagatelle to the **Bagatelle Gardens**. This fragrant park is a favourite spot for romance. The expression *faire la bagatelle* is a quaint euphemism for 'making love'.

Children should head northward to the **Jardin d'Acclimatation** (Metro: Porte Maillot or Sablons). For a small entrance fee, you

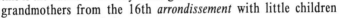

can visit the collection of farm animals and climb, roll, swing, slide, run, crawl and jump on a great collection of playthings. For the price of tokens purchased inside, you can board the miniature train, visit a children's museum, and go on carrousel or mini-motorbike rides. The garden has an old-fashioned atmosphere, reinforced by the people who frequent it: this is the haunt of wealthy white-gloved grandmothers from the 16th *arrondissement* with little children dressed by the top designers.

When you are ready to leave the Bois, amble down the footpath known as the Allée aux Dames which leads away from the Lac Inférieur. This heads over the traffic to the **Fortifications**, named after an archaeological site revealing the last remains of the old city wall. Walk out by the Route des Lacs where it leads to the Place de la Porte de Passy. Cut straight across the wide Boulevard Suchet and veer left on Avenue Ingres into the **Jardins de Ranelagh** (Metro: Ranelagh).

The trees seem to form a vaulting ceiling, green and airy, above the soft sandy floor, transforming the little park into a cathedral. This is where the **Musée Marmottan** (10am–5.30pm, closed Monday) sits discreetly on a corner at 2 Rue Louis Boilly on the north side of the park. The museum is devoted to the work of Impressionist painter Claude Monet. Delicious and colourful as summer itself, the collection includes 100 Monets plus paintings by Gaugin, Sisley, Renoir etc. Downstairs, in a specially designed room, you will encounter the painter's renowned *Water Lilies*, giant canvases painted in his garden in Giverny. Also on display is the Marmottan family's collection of furniture and medieval manuscripts. Oddly enough, the different types of art seem quite at home together in this lovely old building.

Walk out of the triangular-shaped park by its tip on Chaussée

de la Muette and straight ahead through one of the busiest intersections of the 16th, **La Muette** (Metro: La Muette).

A telling story about this wealthy, rather snobbish part of town: when first incorporated into the city, the area was designated district number 13. Well-to-do residents didn't appreciate the unlucky number, and they used their collective political clout to have it changed. The very buildings evoke privilege, with their massive

The Marmottan, for Monet

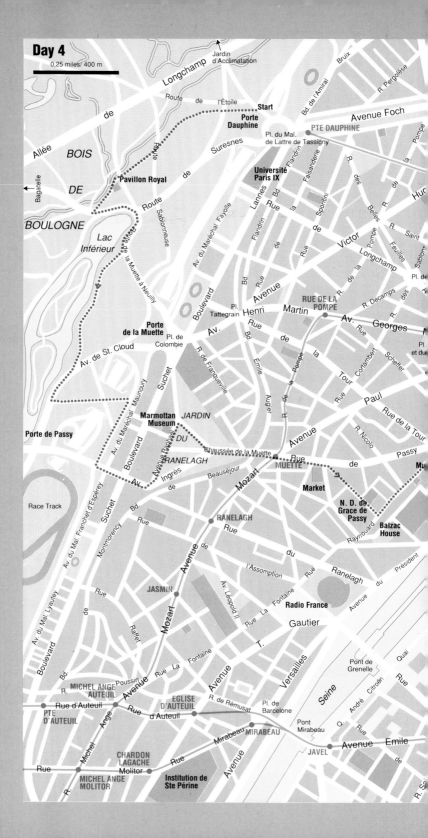

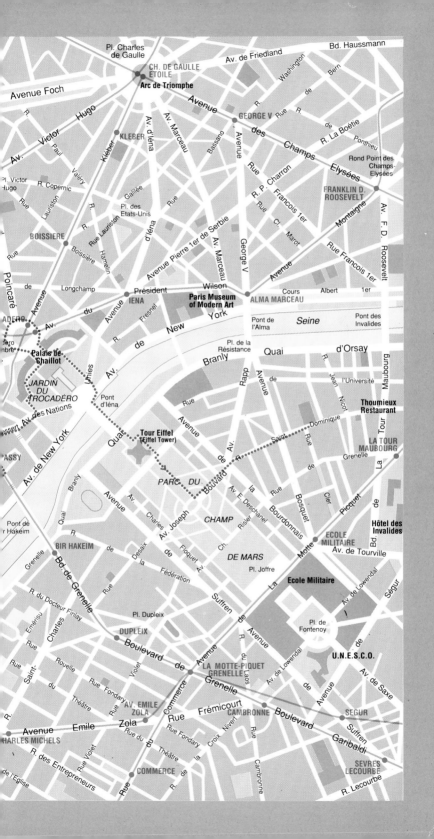

wooden doors, decorative carved facades – the architect's name is often engraved by the doorway – and manicured flower beds. You'll probably see *au pair* girls guiding small children across the street, and maids going shopping with *Madame's* list in hand.

Around **Place de Passy** shopping is busier than ever in the covered market. Here elegant ladies eye ribs of beef and pinch avocados as they plan their dinner parties for the evening ahead. Teenagers turned out in the latest fashions stop in chic little bakeries. Take the pedestrian street which leads off the little square (Passy), the Rue de l'Annonciation, which is lined with a variety of interesting market stalls. Follow it down to the Rue Raynouard (Metro: Passy). At the end of the street, past Notre Dame de Grace de Passy, turn right. You will see **Maison de Balzac** (10am–5.40pm, closed Monday and public holidays) on your left, lending a bit of high-spirited irreverence to this posh neighbourhood. The prolific writer lived here from 1840 to 1847, while revising the 90 volumes of his novel series *La Comédie Humaine*. Downstairs, the complex genealogy of the series' 2,000-odd characters has been mapped out, and Balzac's corrections can be seen in the margins

Balzac's home

of original manuscripts. One look at his cramped writing and the extensive annotations and you understand why typesetters charged double to do his books!

Balzac liked to work from 2am to 5pm. He kept going by drinking copious quantities of black coffee which he concocted himself, which explains the prominent coffee pot. Another feature of the house is a secret exit onto a back street. This was his way of escaping unwelcome callers – particularly debt collectors.

Return on the Rue Raynouard through the apartment blocks to the tiny Passage des Eaux, on the right, which descends steeply to Charles Dickens Square. The **Musée du Vin** (noon–6pm, with its own restaurant) is located here. This simple little museum is very aptly situated, for the cellar cuts into the riverbank hillside that once belonged to the monks of Passy, who made their own wine and stored it there 400 years ago. In the 17th century, the street was crowded with people coming to drink the mineral water flowing from the ground, reputed to have miraculous curative powers. It became a fashionable spot for lovers to meet, and Napoleon himself was seen here frequently.

View from the Totem

During the French Revolution, the last monks were chased from the abbey and the convent was destroyed. None of the other buildings survived after 1906. The cellars were mostly forgotten until the 1960s when the owner of the Eiffel Tower Restaurant started storing his wine there. The present museum opened its doors in 1984.

The exhibits comprise a hodge-podge of tools, containers and wax figures, and the walls are covered with engravings and drawings relating to wine. The boutique has a selection of vintage wines for sale, as well as all sorts of corkscrews, serving baskets, glasses, decanters, books, thermometers, racks – everything to bring out the oenophile in you. And if it is all too much to resist, you can wind up with a little wine-tasting right on the spot.

It is a short walk (or one stop on the Metro from Passy) from the wine museum to **Place du Trocadéro** at the end of Boulevard Delessert. Follow the garden path up to the **Palais de Chaillot** on the hilltop. In the centre of the park, steps and ramps are alive with fountains and kids on roller-skates and skateboards.

The outdoor restaurant on the left is called the **Totem** (tel: 01 47272829), reached by taking the entrance to the Musée de l'Homme. The view over the gardens and across the river to the Eiffel Tower is enough to draw you in. The food is also worthwhile, a cut above

Place du Trocadéro

the usual museum cafeteria. At about 180 Francs per person, it is one of the better deals in the neighbourhood.

The flat terrace between the two wings of Chaillot, lined with golden statuettes, is usually busy with African merchants selling bracelets, leather goods and toys. The curved buildings and monumental landscaping date from the World Fair of 1937, but today the complex is a formidable bastion of culture. It would be impossible to visit all of the exhibition space in one day, but each of these impressive museums deserves a mention, after which you can choose whichever ones suit your particular taste. All are closed on Tuesday.

The **Musée de l'Homme** (Wednesday to Monday, 9.45am–5.15pm, closed Tuesday) is devoted to anthropology. Eskimos, mummies, primitive man, mysterious civilisations, all have a place here. The **Salon de Musique** has a collection of musical instruments through the ages.

Musée des Monuments details

The **Musée des Monuments Français** (Wednesday to Monday 10am–6pm) occupying the north wing of the Palais is another favourite, especially among the French. Roman, Gothic and Renaissance architecture from all over France is represented here. A museum to wander through dreamily, it offers a journey through the French countryside at different points in time.

Also on the hilltop is the **National Popular Theatre** (or Théâtre de Chaillot), which is so big it makes you feel as if you have walked into the belly of a whale. The main house seats an audience of 1,150 people; classical works are usually performed here. The foyer and the smaller house (Gémier) have more offbeat programmes. Finally, the **Musée de la Marine** (Wednesday to Monday 10am–6pm, closed Tuesday), a maritime museum, contains plenty of material designed to appeal to children of all ages.

As you cross the Seine, up looms the **Eiffel Tower**. The 1,050-ft (320-m) tower, once vilified, now reigns as the queen of Parisian monuments. A face-lift in time for its 100th birthday in 1989 coincided with the expiration of a privately held lease. The beauty treatment removed tons of rust and a sagging restaurant. New lights paint the metal lattice-work silver and gold at night.

The glass-walled lift jerks up at an alarming angle. The machinery is unique; a special team of employees does nothing but oversee spare parts, which must be made individually. If you are prepared to go up on foot you can rest on the landings and read about the people who have used the tower for daring exploits, such as riding down on a motorbike. If you take the lift, be prepared to join lengthy queues.

On the first level, an exhibit and short film recount the story of Gustave Eiffel, the tower's architect, and the 1889 World Fair for which it was built. The tower was meant to be temporary, and no one ever intended that it should become the symbol for Paris. In fact it was the advent of radio transmission and the need to site an aerial which gave the tower, the world's highest structure when first built, a reason to stay.

On the top platform is **The Jules Verne** restaurant (which has a private elevator for patrons only). To dine here, you need to make your booking well in advance (tel: 01 45556144). It specialises in fine *cuisine traditionnelle* and its prices are among the highest in Paris, though you are paying as much for the view and the experience as the food. Major credit cards – American Express, Visa, Diner's and Eurocard – are all accepted.

The tower is open until 11pm weekdays; until midnight in July and August. Tickets are a different price for each level. Be prepared to queue for tickets and again for the lifts. The long park stretching away from the riverside and under the tower's splayed feet is the **Parc du Champs de Mars** (Metro: Bir-Hakeim or Ecole Militaire), once a military drill field. At the far end is the 18th-century **Ecole Militaire**, home of France's officer-training academy and several academic institutions.

Walk some distance down the colourful and varied **Rue St Dominique**, which you will find about half-way down the park on the left. At No 79, stop in at **Thoumieux** (tel: 01 47054975). This restaurant is another Parisian landmark (Metro: Invalides). Open daily, its speciality is *cassoulet*, a hearty dish based on white beans and duck which is superb when cooked well, as it is here. Thoumieux's ambience is as appetising as the food – informal and relatively inexpensive.

Alternatively, you may want to take a boat ride along the Seine to Notre Dame from the quay just below the tower, and join up with the tour described in Day 1, *see page 22.*

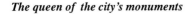

The queen of the city's monuments

PICK & MIX

Morning Itineraries

1. From Rodin to Dior

The 7th and 8th districts of Paris, separated by the Seine, are elegant neighbourhoods. The morning starts amongst the sublime forms in the Rodin Museum then moves north via the Invalides to the river. Afterwards the Grand and Petit Palais, then on to Avenue Montaigne for haute couture.

The **Rodin Museum** (9.30am–5.45pm, winter until 4.45pm, closed Monday) is at 77 Rue de Varenne (Metro: Varenne). In the morning, the rose garden and its still pools are shadowed by the **Hôtel Biron**, built in 1731 as a private residence. August Rodin lived and worked there more than 100 years later, and bequeathed it to the State on the condition that his works be exhibited in the house and park. Though he is now recognised as one of the greatest sculptors of all time, with a technique comparable to that of Michelangelo, Rodin was a figure of controversy in his own lifetime. Some of the early exhibitions of his work brought cries of fraud from

The Rodin Museum, in the Hôtel Biron

'experts' who claimed that his human figures were so anatomically precise they could only have been made by using real bodies to form moulds for casting. In this setting, more than any other, the timeless figures do seem to live and breathe, calling out for caresses.

You enter under the gaze of what is probably Rodin's most famous statue, *The Thinker*, set up high amongst the greenery. To the left, *The Burghers of Calais* re-enact the noble gesture that saved their town from the ravages of the English army in the 14th century. Against the wall, *The Gates of Hell* is a monumental work wreathed with shapes of demons and the damned.

Inside the house, the wooden floors, marble staircase, gilt mirrors and French windows embrace large works, including the prominently displayed *Adam and Eve*, as well as small ones, such as *The Kiss*, a delicate study in white marble. There are works by other artists, including Camille Claudel, Rodin's assistant and mistress. The difficulties of the creative life were multiplied for her as a woman, and she eventually lost her mind and was all but forgotten in a mental institution. The film *Camille*, starring Isabelle Adjani and Gerard Depardieu, created renewed interest in the artist and her relationship with the great master.

Go out the back door and you can wander under the grape arbour and rest on a sunny bench in this remarkable place, so full of peace and so fraught with turbulent feeling.

When you leave the *hôtel*, turn left onto Boulevard des Invalides and walk to **Place Vauban**. Here you have a fine architectural vista offered by the Avenue de Breteuil, stretching out like a green carpet in one direction, and the giant complex known as **Les Invalides** on the other.

The first building that stands out is the golden-domed **Eglise du Dôme**, completely regilded as part of the city's bicentennial facelift in 1989. Therein lies the **Tomb of Napoleon I**, six layers of coffins beneath a

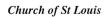

Church of St Louis

sarcophagus of dark red stone. He is kept company by a number of great generals and his son, the ill-fated 'King of Rome'. The decoration inside the church is distinctly military: flags captured from enemies of the Empire are hung on the walls.

The other vast wings of the Invalides were initially built as a veterans' home, but today's old soldiers make do with more ordinary housing, while the buildings house the **Army Museum** (daily 10am–5pm, until 6pm in summer; closed some public holidays) and administrative offices.

The museum is the largest of its kind in the world and exhibits everything from cannons and suits of armour to taxi cabs mobilised for the Marne offensive in World War I. In summer, a nightly sound and light show conjures up the glory days: check the announcements out front for times and languages.

Napoleonic images of grandeur are projected beyond the main entrance across the windswept **Esplanade des Invalides**. Both sides

Cannon detail

of the streets lead away to many government ministries, embassies and official residences. The *ensemble* culminates in the **Pont Alexandre III**, perhaps Paris's most splendid bridge (Metro: Invalides). Built in 1900, the bridge spans the Seine with a single metal arc. The golden statues and distinctive lamp-posts, backed by the domes of the Grand Palais, are typically Parisian.

Crossing the river, you arrive right in the middle of the **Grand Palais** (closed Tuesday) and the **Petit Palais**, museums with permanent and changing exhibits (closed on Monday). Look at the big posters outside to find out what's on. Occasional blockbuster shows bring crowds that form into a long line wrapped all the way around the park. These typical turn-of-the-century wrought-iron and glass 'crystal palaces' were built for the Universal Exhibition of 1900. The gardens that surround them are pleasant and shady; I suggest you take a breather and watch the world go by (Metro: Franklin D Roosevelt or Champs Elysées Clemenceau).

You'll need your breath for exclamations on the last leg of this

Bateau Mouche tour

itinerary: the main branch of 'The Golden Triangle' of shopping streets: **Avenue Montaigne**. Here you can gaze at the displays for Chanel, Cartier, Dior, Vuitton, Nina Ricci, Ungaro, Valentino...and more than your combined credit cards could imagine. Even if you don't venture into the boutiques, you can get an eyeful just strolling down the street, which is kept spotlessly clean and often decorated in holiday style by the classy tenants.

This brings you back to the riverbank at **Alma Marceau** (Metro: Pont d'Alma), where you can stop in a café or brasserie for lunch, or head for a **Bateau Mouche** tour boat just underneath the bridge. You can pick up a snack as you wait for the departure, and spend a pleasant hour off your feet, gliding through the city. Boats leave every 20 minutes or so in summer; at night batteries of lights illuminate the riverside architecture. Don't bother trying to listen to the static and crackle of the multilingual, taped commentary, just sit back and look. Sure, it's touristy, but even nonchalant Parisians enjoy the unique view from the water.

Pont Alexandre III, the most splendid bridge in Paris

2. Père Lachaise

This suggestion for a peaceful morning in eastern Paris takes you to a resting place for the famous and a Parisian village.

Those who know it love to return, and some who go there never leave – such as Frédéric Chopin, Molière, Rossini, and more recent luminaries including Edith Piaf, Gertrude Stein, Oscar Wilde, Jim Morrison and Yves Montand. The place, of course, is the **Père Lachaise Cemetery**, in eastern Paris, the city's largest and loveliest burial ground (Metro: Père Lachaise).

At the main entrance on Boulevard de Menilmontant, visitors can pick up a map pinpointing the more famous graves, and the small bookstore also sells a surprising variety of guides to the cemetery. Indeed, most of the people wandering about seem more curious than bereaved.

At first glance, this older part of the cemetery near the entrance appears to make use of above-ground burial, but look closely and you'll see that the tiny houses in this city of the dead are actually small chapels, often in disrepair. Walk up Avenue Principale and turn right to find the monument marking the grave of Héloïse and Abelard. She was a student of the controversial theologian in the 12th century, and secretly became his wife. Her father's fury separated them, he (castrated) in a monastery

Chopin's tomb

and she in a convent, but they left their letters to posterity, professing a pure and faithful love.

Make your way along the shady paths to the chapel on the hilltop for a view over the stalwart chestnut trees, spreading like guardian

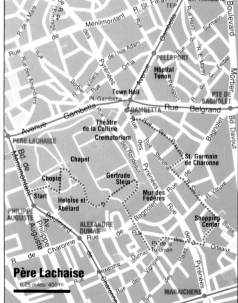

spirits over the myriad monuments. You may see the benches occupied by old women feeding the many cats who make their homes amongst the monuments.

Others come to visit the grave of Allan Kardec, spiritualist, and leave odd mementos or practise bizarre rites in front of his tomb.

Of historic interest is the **Mur des Fédérés**, located at the back of the cemetery in its eastern corner where grotesque and striking war memorials spring from the

Rue St Blaise

earth. The wall was where the last of the anarchist rebels of the *Commune de Paris,* a courageous uprising against Prussian domination in 1871, were lined up and shot. The bullet holes are still visible. Also in this top corner is the Jardin du Souvenir, with many monuments commemorating the dead of World War II, including some dedicated to the victims of Auschwitz, Ravensbruck, Buchenwald and others. There are also monuments to different members of the French Resistance. If you are especially interested in this period, you may be lucky and come across war veterans or historians here.

Leave the quiet behind slowly, exiting at this corner down the steps onto **Rue de la Réunion** (named after the Indian Ocean island which is a French territory), a street more full of baby strollers than cars. This is the sort of neighbourhood where people close up the shop and set off home for lunch and a snooze complete with a *baguette* of bread under the arm.

Keep going across Rue Bagnolet to **Place de la Réunion**, which looks as if it has been picked up and transported from a much smaller town in France – or even directly from the tropics, as the local African community adds a colourful dimension to the tiny circle and park. It may be rather ramshackle and not particularly elegant, but this is just as much the true Paris as the world famous downtown boulevards.

Continue through this neighbourhood of small shops and furniture craftsmen down the Rue des Orteaux and just under the old train line into Rue du Clos. This takes you to **Le Village St Blaise**, tucked discreetly into this eastern end of Paris (Metro: Porte de Montreuil). Part of the neighbourhood is a modern public housing development and shopping centre with a purple colour scheme. The quality and originality of the architecture and planning belie the 'moderate rent' nature of the housing.

Turn left and walk up Rue St Blaise. Up here is a good find for lunch, an Algerian restaurant called **Le Village de Paris** (24 Rue St Blaise, tel: 01 43566663). *Couscous*, the main item on the menu, has become very popular in Paris, and not only among the large North African population. This family restaurant is warm and homely. Big dishes are brought out to the table for you to garnish your plate as you choose with a selection of exotic appetisers. Then follows the *couscous:* four varieties of fluffy semolina, a bowl of piping hot vegetables and sauce; a little tub of hot pepper sauce for spice; and either mutton, chicken or beef.

After the meal, pass around the plate of fresh dates. If you like North African food, head directly here, you can't find better, and you can't beat the prices (150 Francs gets you any dish on the menu).

The street has a number of other possibilities that may tempt you back another time, including a dainty tea room for delicate eaters further down (**Le Damier**).

Watching over Rue St Blaise, its single rose window like a benevolent eye, is **St Germain de Charonne**, whose country-church character suits the neighbourhood well. This church is so popular for weddings that Parisians sign up a year in advance for the pleasure of saying *oui* at the altar and having their wedding pictures taken out front. Walk up the steps on its left side, and take a look at the cemetery – quite a contrast to Père Lachaise.

From here the Rue des Prairies and Rue des Pyrénées will take you back to **Place Gambetta**, the heart of the 20th *arrondissement*, and the Metro.

3. Shopping Tour

Looking for a special gift? Feeling guilty about leaving the kids behind? Ready to brave the fashion boutiques? Follow this trail. If you're a window shopper only, the route can easily be completed in a morning, but if you intend to go on a spree, it could take a whole day!

There's one Metro station in Paris that everyone seems to pass through regularly, and it bears the name of the famous building above it, the **Opéra**. It's a lively neighbourhood, the hub of the Grands Boulevards, and a business centre to banks, travel companies, and the nearby Stock Exchange (La Bourse).

If you need to replenish your wallet before your spree, stop off first at **American Express**, on Rue Scribe, with many services for travellers including banking and foreign exchange. Or if you're in a hurry and have cash, try the automatic money exchange machine at

Buy a bit of elegance

the BNP **Bank** right on the Place de l'Opéra. Twenty-four hours a day, you can slip your own currency in the slot and get Francs in return, or use your ATM or credit card. Various travel and ticket agents for tours and shows are here and the surrounding streets, so it's a good opportunity to line something up for the evening or for another day.

Start your tour proper at the **Palais Garnier** (open 10am–4.30pm) as the Opéra building is officially known. This 'wedding cake' was completed in 1875, the crowning achievement of the plan designed by Haussmann to open up the centre of Paris.

You can walk into the vaulting foyer for a glimpse of the eclectic décor, and on days when no rehearsal is in progress, you can go into the theatre itself. A splendid surprise awaits you overhead: painter **Marc Chagall's ceiling**, a frolicsome work in blue and pearl tones, in striking contrast to the sombre red and gold opulence of the hall. Guided tours of the Opéra (in French) are conducted at 10.45am Monday to Saturday.

Just across the street is the **Grand Hotel,** and its sidewalk café, the **Café de la Paix,** one of the most celebrated in Paris. This is a prime spot for indulging in the art of seeing and being seen, or completing a *rendezvous*. The expansive (and expensive!) café, taking up a whole corner of the Place de l'Opéra, is not the place to go when you're in a hurry, but, as its name suggests, a venue for a moment of peace in the midst of the crowd. If you really need to get out of the fray, there's a cosy bar tucked away on the far side of the main hall of the

hotel. The bartenders there have invented a few special cocktails that you won't forget.

Revived and refreshed, head for *Les Grands Magasins*. These department stores sprang up in Paris during the 19th century and have been popular among Parisians and visitors ever since. On Boulevard Haussmann you'll find the **Galeries Lafayette** first of all, famous its sparkling jewel-box interior. Walk in and orient yourself by heading for the central escalators and the store directory in French and English, plus a bilingual hostess who can help you find that perfect gift. Other services at the store include a fashion consultant, currency exchange, and duty free forms for recovering sales taxes at the airport. Fashion is the biggest seller here, whether it's off-the-rack designer or the Galeries' own label. Beautifully made accessories like stockings, scarves and headwear can suddenly seem like essential items of clothing. Its lingerie department is legendary.

Across the street is a branch of **Marks and Spencer**, the British chain store, which seems just as popular as its French cousins – even among visiting British for some reason. And another block down is **Printemps**, which advertises itself as 'the most Parisian department store'. It certainly is the most beautiful inside: the domed ceiling built in 1923 is now classed as a historic monument. The perfume department is supposed to have the largest selection of lotions and potions in Paris. There are make-up demonstrations and fashion shows scheduled almost every day of the week, and there are the same services for English-speaking tourists as in the Galeries Lafayette.

The street outside the two stores takes up the overflow of commerce and all along the pavements you'll be entertained by fast and furious sales pitches for revolutionary cookware, two-for-one deals of a lifetime, and the latest development in travel irons. There are plenty of odd-lots and bargains for those who can withstand the pressure of the crowd flowing by.

Jump out of the main stream of traffic onto the pedestrian **Rue de Caumartin** (Metro: Havre-Caumartin). There is more room to breathe on this street, bordered by smaller shops and the 18th-

Galeries Lafayette, where fashion is the biggest seller

century **St Louis d'Antin church**. Free organ concerts are regularly scheduled on weekends; leaflets inside the main entrance give the dates. More spontaneous street music concerts are likely to be in progress at any time.

But if you're not ready to interrupt your shopping, or if you still haven't found what you're looking for, continue your shopping tour back down Rue Tronchet and Rue Vignon, which lead from St Lazare to the Place de la Madeleine. **Rue Vignon** in particular is worth a meander. It has smaller boutiques that may not carry the big designer names found on the Avenue Montaigne but are nonetheless filled with interesting ideas and prices. For unusual little gifts or souvenirs, I can recommend **La Maison du Miel** (24 Rue Vignon), offering French honey in pretty little pots and other beautifully packaged products such as soaps and shampoos.

The monumental church in the centre of **Place de la Madeleine** (Metro: La Madeleine) is not very welcoming. More rewarding are the window displays at **Fauchon**, which confirm France's reputed supremacy in the art of presenting food. You

The Ritz Hotel

can eat here *sur le pouce* (informally), a favourite lunchtime option among people who work in the neighbourhood: just point at whichever delicacy you fancy behind the glass cases; a member of staff will pile a portion onto a plate and you can eat it (standing up) at the counter.

If you would rather sit with a picnic than eat on your feet, head for the nearby Tuileries after a stop at one of the other exotic food shops on the Place de la Madeleine. Try **Hédiard**, where you can fill your basket with caviar, tropical fruits, and a vintage wine. The staff will wrap your purchases in chic black and red paper and tie them up with ribbon.

The **Rue Faubourg St Honoré** and **Rue St Honoré** continue the chic shopping. These streets are the traditional (if somewhat outmoded) address for major designers like **Hermès** and **Gucci**. Just around the corner is the **Place Vendôme**, elegantly symmetrical and home to the Ritz Hotel and **Cartier** jewellers, whose major outlet is nearby on Rue de la Paix.

If you've still got money left at the end of your day, why not enjoy tea at the **Ritz** (proper attire is required), owned by the Egyptian owner of London's Harrods, Mohammed Al Fayed, and engraved on many people's memory as the hotel from which the Princess of Wales set out on that fatal car journey in 1997. If you feel you deserve something a little stronger than tea, you can adjourn to the hotel's **Hemingway Bar**, named after the writer who made it his hangout.

Afternoon Itineraries

· 4. Montmartre and Pigalle

Montmartre, perched on a steep hill on the northern rim of Paris, is a legend in itself. It seems to have its own history apart from the city below, its own famous citizens, and its own traditions in entertainment and art. The Sacré Coeur Basilica, a landmark which can be observed from all over the city, is the central tourist site, but not really the heart of its neighbourhood. Be warned: free maps don't show the narrow streets of this itinerary.

I should just say that Montmartre is almost always very crowded with tourists. But, surprisingly, a walk of a few blocks away from the central Place du Tertre brings you to quiet streets where stairs tumble down to the city below, quiet as the cats prowling about. If stairs and steep hills are too much for you, I'd recommend the Montmartrobus, a special bus line that runs between Pigalle and the hilltop. For the cost of one Metro ticket for a one-way trip, it is the best tour deal in town.

Montmartre is known for its artists

Much the same route is also covered by a miniature train (Le Petit Train de Montmartre); the latter is cute, but no great improvement and more expensive.

Start the itinerary at the **Place d'Anvers** (Metro: Anvers). Follow the signs to the *Funiculaire* that lead you up the Rue Steinkerque. The street is lined with fabric and clothes shops. If you have an eye for that sort of thing, there are nice bits of velvet ribbon, fancy buttons and trims, something to take home. You can also find the lacy curtains that are so typically Parisian, with unusual motifs and designs.

At the top of the street, with Montmartre's white basilica rising above you, turn right to walk down to the **Marché St**

Pierre. This 19th-century covered marketplace has recently changed its vocation. It is now home to the **Primitive Art Museum** (Musée d'Art Naïf Max Fourny; Tuesday to Sunday 10am–6pm except some public holidays, closed Monday), which presents works by artists from around the world, painting in the colourful, magical style that Rousseau made famous. It also runs children's workshops, and the bookshop has an original selection of books, cards and ideas for manual activities for children. Look out for postcards which you can cut out into earrings.

Above the green park bordering the Place St Pierre looms the **Sacré Coeur** ('sacred heart') **Basilica**, which was built a mere century ago – small potatoes in this city. Its construction came on the heels of the Commune de Paris uprising against Prussian domination in 1871. The uprising took its inspiration and strength from Montmartre and its anarchist population, who resisted to the last. It was French regular troops who betrayed the *Communards*, executing 25,000 of them in the final weeks of battle.

The church was built in appeasement for the bloodshed, and so has never been well-loved by local residents, known as *Montmartrois*. To this day, it is often mocked in cabaret songs on the hilltop (locally known as *La Butte*).

Climb the switchback stairway, or relax in the **Funicular railway** (use one Metro ticket) to reach the terrace in front of Sacré Coeur. From here you have a splendid view over the city, and coin-

Sacré Coeur Basilica, a Parisian landmark

operated telescopes to help you pick out your favourite places. Look straight out directly south into the centre of Paris, and you should easily distinguish the brightly-coloured Pompidou Centre and the two square towers of Notre Dame, which stand out from the otherwise remarkably low-rise and uniform city centre. This vista is just at the opposite side of Paris from the panorama seen at the top of the Montparnasse Tower (*Day 1*). The Tower is off to the right, black and solitary on the skyline.

Now walk around to the right behind the church. It is like going behind a curtain and discovering a magical theatre set. Follow the lane round to the left and the **Place du Tertre** greets you with strings of bright lights and swirls of colourful people. You will return to the square later. Battling through the crowds towards the *point de vue* on the corner of Rue Poulbot you will find the new Espace Montmartre (10am–6pm), home to over 300 works by **Salvador Dalí**, and its popular shop.

Stroll down Rue du Mont Cenis; leaving the crowd behind, and take a left on Rue Cortot. No 6 was the house Eric Satie lived in while composing his delightful piano pieces. The painter Utrillo, who captured so many of *La Butte's* houses and cafés in his work, also lived on this street, with his mother, artist Suzanne Valadon.

At No 12 is the **Musée de Montmartre** (11am–6pm, closed Monday) settled in an 18th-century manor house along with the **Montmartre Cultural Centre**. Its windows overlook the **Montmartre Vineyards** and Rue St Vincent. Every October, there is a big harvest celebration here.

Obviously, given the size of the vineyard, there is not a lot of

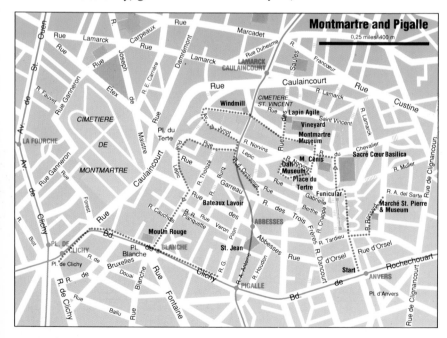

Place du Tertre, Montmartre

wine bottled, and its value is more sentimental than gustatory. But it is a great source of pride to the *Montmartrois*, proving that these folks still have a strong community spirit. On the lower floors of the museum, you can see recreations of the study of composer and violinist Gustave Charpentier, and a reconstruction of Utrillo's favourite café, l'Abreuvoir. The graceful garden setting and the care with which original objects have been preserved and presented make this the best museum to visit in Montmartre. It sums up the long history and special character of the 'village' well.

Go to the end of Rue Cortot and turn right onto Rue des Saules. The vineyards are visible from down here for those who didn't go into the museum, with the Montmartre Cemetery behind its wall diagonally across from the vines. A bit further down is **Le Lapin Agile** (22 Rue des Saules, Metro: Lamarck-Caulaincourt), an old-fashioned cabaret which opens at 9pm, and the last show ends at 2am. The entrance price gets you a spot on a long wooden bench by a scarred table, and a little glass of cherries in *eau-de-vie*. All night long, guests are treated to 'songs, humour and poetry', in the tradition established here by Aristide Bruant, who was immortalised by the Toulouse-Lautrec portrait showing him in his perpetual black hat and cape. Many of the roving performers sing songs he composed as they make the rounds of cabarets on the *Butte*. Le Lapin sounds quaint, but it is also fast-paced, and you'd have to have good knowledge of French to appreciate it.

Back up the hill, the restaurant **La Maison Rose** on the corner was the subject of the painting that brought fame to Utrillo. Left at the Maison Rose leads to an elegant corner called the **Allée des Brouillards**. Ivy-covered gates stand before snug houses and their neat gardens. The **Château des Brouillards** (Castle

Le Lapin Agile, old-fashioned cabaret

of the Mists) stands opposite, in a small park. The house was built in 1772 by an actor from the Comédie Française, and several artists lived in it during the years that followed. Now boarded up, it is a spooky place, haunted by the souls of poets.

Go down the steps of Rue Girardon to Avenue Junot. Follow the curving Avenue Junot back up to Girardon and Rue Lepic; at the crossroads stands the **Moulin de la Galette**. The windmill was made into a dance hall in the 19th century, and celebrated in a painting by Renoir. Vincent Van Gogh lived with his brother in a pretty little house at No 54 Rue Lepic.

Go across Lepic into a little alley called Rue d'Orchampt, and

follow it round. At the end there is a row of artists' studios that look much like the old **Bateau Lavoir** did when Picasso and Braque painted there. The site of their Montmartre studios is around the corner on **Place Emile Goudeau** (Metro: Abbesses).

Of course, many of the famous artists who lived and loved in Montmartre – Picasso, Apollinaire, Matisse, Toulouse-Lautrec, Marie Laurencin, to name only a few – were also great *bons vivants*. A good time is still on the agenda, and to make the most of your night out, I have three suggestions to suit your style.

Back in Place du Tertre I recommend **A La Mère Catherine** (on the square, tel: 01 46063269). This is the classic French restaurant. The décor is dignified and warm, the menu is kept simple and inviting. The years haven't changed much about this place at all; it's not unusual to see three generations sitting at the same table, and none of them looks out of place. (Expect to pay about 150 Francs per person.)

Another more informal option is **Tartempion** (tel: 01 46061040), on Rue du Mont Cenis, serving plain fare and tasty desserts at moderate prices (100–150 Francs). On a warm night you can sit outdoors on the terrace with a view of the street as it abruptly ends in a stairway, and the city lights floating in space beyond.

After dinner, I suggest you stay on the *Butte* and head for **La Bohème du Tertre** (tel: 01 46065169). You can't miss this brightly lit cabaret on a corner of Place du Tertre. Head for the back room where musicians play traditional dance music (polka, waltz, and a Charleston or two). The crowd really gets going with French drinking songs and old songs about Montmartre. Order a bottle of wine and dance and sing until 2am.

Alternatively, there are famous and racier venues nearby. Come down off the hilltop and out of the shadow of the church to head for the naughtier regions of lower Montmartre and Pigalle. Take the twisty Rue Lepic all the way to Place Blanche (Metro: Blanche), where you will find the unmistakable **Moulin Rouge**. Skip the dinner show

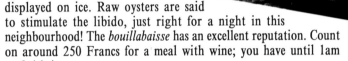

here, the food is dull and the prices high, but take a look at the photos for fun, and buy a ticket for later if you're interested. The Moulin has been showing feathers and skin for 100 years now, so must be doing something right. Continue on down the sexy Boulevard de Clichy to the **Place de Clichy** (Metro: Place de Clichy) and the restaurant **Charlot Roi des Coquillages** (tel: 01 53204800). The speciality here is, of course, seafood, enticingly displayed on ice. Raw oysters are said to stimulate the libido, just right for a night in this neighbourhood! The *bouillabaisse* has an excellent reputation. Count on around 250 Francs for a meal with wine; you have until 1am to finish it.

Also on Place de Clichy is **Wepler** (tel: 01 45225329), the oyster bar and restaurant favoured by author Henry Miller when he sowed his wild oats in this part of town. Open until 1.30am, Wepler is similar in price to Charlot.

After dinner, you can backtrack to Blanche and continue all the way to **Pigalle** (Metro: Pigalle), popularly known to WWII soldiers as 'Pig Alley'. Along the way, there are plenty of strip shows with hawkers to lure you inside. The entrance fee to these places is next to nothing, but the drinks served inside are obligatory and extremely expensive.

Pigalle is changing all the time; **Folies Pigalle**, for example, has gone from sex show to alternative theatre to music hall. Rock clubs offer a different brand of entertainment and attract a new crowd. **La Locomotive** (90 Blvd de Clichy) goes full steam ahead until 5.30am. It is a lot bigger than the Folies, has two separate discos, two bars, a video room and live music. And when the club closes, you can go back up the hill for sunrise!

One hundred years of feathers, skin and sin

5. By Canal to La Villette

The canals of Paris? Yes indeed, and although there are no singing gondoliers, there are locks and barges, and a very particular urban landscape. What used to be a trade lifeline has now been restored for leisure use. Discover this surprising waterway, and the modern new museum complex that has been built along its banks, Parc de la Villette. This is a good itinerary for children, particularly if you are tired of walking.

Redevelopment of the area around La Bastille began with the improvement of the **Arsenal Marina** (Metro: Bastille). The Marina was once a very active commercial shipping port; adjacent to the Seine it joins the **Canal St Martin** leading eastward out of the city. At Bastille, the canal goes underground, emerging again beyond Place de la République. Board the **Canauxrama Tour Boat** (tel: 01 42391500) at Arsenal Marina, on the level of No 50 Blvd de la Bastille, for a three-hour journey eastward. Departures are at 9.30am and 2.30pm daily and the commentary is only in French.

Napoleon built the canal partly to get more water into the city centre and thus earn the citizens' affection; in those days average daily consumption was 1 litre (just over 2 pints) per person, as opposed to 200 litres today. As you glide under the city, the canal is lit by sidewalk gratings sending eerie shafts of light down to the water. The different colours of mortar indicate where restoration work has been carried out; the area directly overhead has been untouched since the canal was built. Classical music from the boat echoes through the tunnel.

Arsenal Marina

The Géode –
circular projection screen

At Quai Valmy and Quai de Jemmapes, you emerge in trees and gardens and yet another unique Parisian landscape. Wait patiently at the locks; note how the moss on the canal walls often hides fresh water mussels.

On the left bank, your guide will point out the **Hôtel du Nord**, and play part of the soundtrack. This was the setting for a French movie of the same name. When the hotel was recently slated for demolition, neighbours and cinephiles protested so strongly that the famous facade was saved.

Near the **Bassin de la Villette**, warehouses and cafés cater mainly to the leisure boaters on the canal. Some of the industrial space here has been reclaimed by artists' cooperatives as studio space and undoubtedly this neighbourhood is in for some big changes in the years ahead. Just beyond the port, the canal divides into the Canal St Denis and the Canal de l'Ourcq, two working waterways.

This is the end of your boat ride. What you see all around you now is known as the **Parc de la Villette** (Metro: Porte de Pantin). It is a big cultural complex created in 1986 on the site of the city's former cattle market. The market building itself, a fine example of 19th-century iron architecture to the right of the canal, is now an exhibition space, **La**

Walkway at La Villette

Grande Halle. Exhibits here range from the prestigious and often controversial Paris Biennale contemporary art show to the International Architectural Fair, and even presentations of fashion collections. There is a small space called **La Maison de la Villette** with a permanent exhibit on the history of La Villette and the market.

On the left of the canal, the **Géode**, a polished steel sphere that plays weird music, looks like something from outer space that just landed in a pond. Inside, the hemispheric theatre has one of the world's largest projection screens and dizzily slanted seating. Movies are made specially for these huge screens. Outside, photographers try to capture its mystery on film.

Reflected in the shiny steel is the **Cité des Sciences et de l'industrie** (Tuesday to Sunday 10am–6pm, Sunday 10am–7pm, closed Monday). It takes hours to see the whole thing, and the entrance fees for its various sections – waived if you have a museums pass – are relatively high. Even if you don't visit the whole thing, you can walk in the main hall for free and look at the exhibits on the ground floor.

Brochures and cassette guides in English are available. La Villette is devoted to science. One of the best parts is a big room for children (of all ages) where visitors participate in experiments using soap bubbles, mirrors, electricity, magnets and tricks of perspective. There is a jet pack simulator for armchair astronauts.

Other exhibits in the museum cover the universe, the origins of life, the underwater world, plant life, and there are even animal robots in a cybernetic zoo. At every turn hands-on computer terminals inform and amuse.

Short films are shown in different areas, and the ultra-modern **Planetarium** runs several programmes a day (there is an extra charge; get your tickets as soon as you arrive – they go fast).

In the park next to the northern bridge is a big, grey, square and solid-looking tent. This is the **Zénith Concert Hall**, which can seat up to 6,300 people. It has excellent acoustics and modern facilities, and is often booked for rock music.

La Villette is not the place for haute cuisine, but there's a selection of cafés and burger bars dotted through the park and in the city of sciences.

To get back into town from here, you can take the Metro from Porte de la Villette. Alternatively, a pleasant route is to take bus No 75, which goes right back to the Pompidou Centre and Hôtel de Ville. Pick it up at the **Place de la Porte de Pantin**, which you reach by turning left at the road entrance to the Grande Halle and walking up to the big roundabout. Like most of the Parisian buses,

Passing time in the park

it runs until about 8.30pm; after that, you'll have to look for a taxi or use the Metro.

The bus route takes you past the hilly park of the **Buttes Chaumont**, built in an old quarry and planted in the English romantic style with trees, islands, and a little Greek temple just peeping through the trees atop its knoll.

After this, the bus passes **Place du Colonel Fabien**, and the headquarters of the French Communist Party, designed by Brazilian architect Oscar Niemeyer. It goes back down to Place de la République and from there turns into the Marais district past the Pompidou Centre and on to the Hôtel de Ville. A short trip down busy Rue de Rivoli and the bus driver takes a break at the **Pont Neuf Bridge**; the name means 'New Bridge', but in fact it is the oldest in town, and one of the most remarkable. From the riverside, note the hundreds of faces carved along the side, each one unique.

6. The New Louvre

You may be startled to see references to the 'New Louvre' or Le Grand Louvre. What happened to the old Louvre? The answer is: a lot! Astonishing changes have been made, not without controversy but certainly with great success. The world's largest museum is still labyrinthine, but a joy to discover for old hands as well as first-time visitors. And only the French would be so bold as to completely re-do their major world museum.

Le Grand Louvre (9am–6pm Thursday to Monday; closed Tuesday; 9am–9.45pm Wednesday; the Richelieu Wing is open until 9.45 on Monday) is the name ex-President François Mitterrand gave his vast restructuring project. The first, much-delayed, step involved prying the Finance Ministry out of its privileged premises in one wing of the palace. The second major step commissioned the Chinese-American architect IM Pei to create a new entrance and orientation centre.

In the Louvre

His design is already world-famous, and although not to everyone's taste it will certainly become part of the architectural legend of Paris. The large glass **Pyramid** rises in the middle of the **Cour Napoléon**. Around it are three smaller pyramids. The area between them is accented by flat, triangular basins in dark stone, raised slightly above the level of the ground. Fountains in these pools complete the composition.

The 'landscape', as Pei calls it, in the tradition of landscape artist Le Nôtre, was designed to bring light into the museum entrance below, and it also succeeds in lightening the whole courtyard and the stone façades surrounding it.

Inside the Louvre pyramid

Thoughtful use of materials and colours allows the sky and water to become elements in illusionistic space. The glass was specially developed and polished twice in France and England. It is held in place by stainless steel nodes and cables. The result is light and sparkling, a balance of reflection and transparency weighed against the thick stone facade of the old palace, which is heavy with centuries of history. This is the **main entrance** to the museum, but you may be able to dodge any queues by using the Richelieu Passage, off Rue de Rivoli and the Place du Palais Royal. Go through the revolving door and turn down the spiral staircase. The central pillar is an ingenious elevator. This is the **Hall Napoléon** reception area. The din of milling visitors sounds like a swimming pool, but the museum is not overbearing and has plenty of space.

The new museum services located here are excellent. Ticket windows, the information desk, a bookshop, the rest rooms, and the cafeteria are all easy to find and reach – already a big improvement over the old Louvre! A sit-down restaurant and a sandwich bar provide alternatives for hungry and thirsty visitors. A wall of screens lists the day's exhibits and activities, and rooms which may be temporarily closed. You will also find a post office, money changing facilities, a cloak room and even an infirmary on this level. The bookshop sells not only postcards and prints, but 15,000 books and periodicals in many languages, with a good selection for children. Casts of art works, jewellery and other gift items are also on sale.

Elegant and light

English cassette tours are available, and a six-minute film presentation on some of the major works can be seen in the reception. You can take a tour with a guide.

When construction began on the new Louvre, major archaeological research was carried out. The fruits of these efforts are now on display in an underground exhibition area called the **Medieval Louvre**. Drawings and scale models show the Louvre at different stages of its career, and reveal how many transformations it had known prior to today. Walk around the ancient walls and most of the medieval fortress, past the towers that were once the gates to the city. The architectural prowess used to display the old foundations so effectively is breathtaking.

There is an exhibition of some of the artifacts uncovered, including many ceramic pieces. The most splendid find was certainly the **Helmet of Charles VI**, found in barely recognisable bits and artfully reproduced. It is on display in the **Salle Saint Louis**, perhaps the most impressive part of the newly opened area.

The Louvre, with its new openings and additions, is now bigger

The Louvre's most famous portrait

than ever, and it is impossible not to get lost. No matter which way you turn in the museum, you always seem to end up in the Egyptian Antiquities! However, like Alice in Wonderland, visitors need only wander at random to discover many marvels. The Pyramid, visible from many different angles through tall windows, and the free handbook from the foyer will help keep you orientated. On the ground floor, the **Oriental, Egyptian, Greek** and **Roman Antiquities** were the first items to be displayed. Many were brought back from Napoleon's campaigns.

The Egyptian section has, of course, mummies and cult objects, busts and statues of ancient rulers. This famous collection enables scholars to trace the whole development of Egyptian civilisation from prehistory to the Christian era.

Two very famous ladies grace the Greek and Roman rooms: *Venus de Milo* and *Winged Victory*. Their celebrity has somewhat overshadowed the rest. Vast, sunny and quiet, the proportions of the rooms are well suited to the pieces. Although the outstanding part of this section is made up of sculpture, there are also bronzes, decorative and useful objects, tools, jewellery and bas-reliefs. Many are details taken from the city's various eras.

The second major section of the Louvre collection is **paintings**. The collection spans all the European schools, from the 13th to the 17th centuries, and they are displayed on the upper floors. Two-thirds of the paintings are French, and include works by 17th- and 18th-century artists such as de la Tour, Poussin, Watteau and Fragonard; all to be visited in the **Grande Galérie**. This section's most famous resident is, of course, the *Mona Lisa*, in the company of an impressive gathering of other works by Leonardo da Vinci. Masterpieces by Raphael, Titian, and Veronese compete for the visitor's eye in these rooms.

Other crowd stoppers in this section include some of the large paintings in the **Pavillon Denon**: *Napoleon Crowning Josephine* (David), *The Great Odalisque* (Ingres), *The Raft of the Medusa* (Géricault), and the revolutionary and inspiring *Liberty Leading the People* (Delacroix).

A place for study

The third section is known as **Objets d'Art** (Richelieu and Sully wings) and has on display furniture, jewellery and small statuary, much of which was confiscated from the royalty at the time of the Revolution. **Apollo's Gallery** (Galérie d'Apollon) is a beautiful room with an intricate ceiling that was painted by Delacroix. Glass cases display the remaining pieces of the Crown Jewels of France. The reputed Crown of St Louis sits alongside Napoleon's coronation headgear. Numerous gem-encrusted and golden objects glitter beneath the guard's watchful eye. Less overwhelming – but just as admirable – is the collection of tapestries, furniture and clocks.

The great redistribution of paintings in the Louvre, now that more space is available, will take several years to complete. Eventually, paintings will be rearranged in a more chronological perspective, and according to national schools. Already works which were previously not hung for lack of space are on public view. In the new top-floor rooms, these include *The History of Alexander* by Le Brun, a series of huge paintings that have been rolled up for almost 30 years.

Other works will be shown on a rotating basis as the program of redistribution is carried out. So even Louvre veterans should be prepared for some surprises.

7. La Défense

An afternoon at the avant-garde business district on the west side of the city centre. La Défense epitomises French commitment to grand and futuristic projects.

Take the RER line A to La Défense, the same line which – on the other side of Paris – travels out to Disneyland Paris. The two venues have something in common, because in both you emerge into completely new worlds, worlds which are hard to believe in when you come straight from the historic heart of Paris.

At La Défense the station exits emerge into the **Les Quatre Temps** commercial centre, with some 250 shops and restaurants in a rather un-Parisian shopping-mall style. Head for the daylight, following signs to the **Grande Arche**. This latter building is at the top of the long flight of courtyards up the centre of the district, and is very simplistic in its architecture. Climb the steps, then stop and turn after the last step to witness one of the most magnificent – and oldest – pieces of city planning in the world stretching below you. The Grande Arche is at the end of an axis that runs straight as a die to the Arc de Triomphe, continues down the Champs-Elysées, through Concorde and ends at the Arc de Triomphe du Carrousel, just in front of the Louvre. This axis hasn't stopped growing: there are plans to extend it further west. Turning around again, go into the open centre of the Grande Arche, from where there are lifts to the top (April to October 10am–7pm daily; November to March 11am–6pm, 10am on the weekend; closed on Tuesday).

You may notice that the Grande Arche is slightly at an angle to the axis. This is not a creative spin by Danish architect Johan Otto von Spreckelsen, it is thanks to problems in siting the foundations. Even on the calmest of days the Grande Arche whispers with sea-noises, and it emanates a bewitching sense of peace.

Most of the buildings of La Défense are headquarters, and are often clearly labelled as so. About three-quarters of the top 20 French companies have their main offices here, as do a dozen or so of the top 50 companies in the world. And even though the *Grand Projet* of La Défense was officially completed in 1988 after 20 years, many of the original buildings are now being replaced with bigger, better and more advanced constructions. In all, some 140,000 people work at La Défense for around 1,300 companies, and the area is also home to more than 30,000 residents who live mainly on the outer sides or behind, in the landscaped park district.

On a fine day La Défense is a pleasant place to be. Wander down from the Grande Arche and look at the sculptures there are over 70 signed pieces on the premises – including works by Miró and César. Half-way along the route, the fountains are orchestrated into water-ballets at certain times of the day. On a wet day the weather can turn the open area into a deserted canyon of architecture; you could do worse than scurry into the **Dôme IMAX**, a hemispherical cinema, or the **Automobile Museum**'s display of more than 100 vintage cars. There is also a programme of arts for which you will need to consult the local press.

The Grande Arche at La Défense

EXCURSIONS

The region immediately surrounding the city of Paris is called the *Ile de France*, and is rich in history and culture. Some of the most popular spots are also the most accessible, and typical French countryside is never far away. The following destinations can easily visited in a day. If you leave Paris before noon, you can be back in time for dinner.

8. Versailles

Versailles is top on the list of what tourists want to see outside of the city. Rapid transit RER line C, with stops all along the left bank of the Seine, will take you there in a jiffy. When you exit at the Versailles station, signs clearly indicate how to walk or take a bus to the château, which is only a short distance away.

(The inside of the palace is open: Tuesday to Sunday 2 May to 30 September 9am–6.30pm, 1 October to 30 April Tuesday to Sunday 9am–5.30pm; closed Monday. The vast gardens are open from early morning to nightfall. A guided tour of the palace – unaccompanied visits are not allowed – takes about an hour, but you may have to wait in line almost as long.)

It took 50 years to complete Louis XIV's – the Sun King's – plans for this sumptuous palace, a building that gives meaning to the

The grand facade of Versailles

A Versailles clock

word *grandeur*. In fact, this insensitive display of wealth on the king's part foreshadowed the French Revolution. Because he hated Paris and the unpredictable Parisians, and was jealous of the luxurious castle at Vaux-le-Vicomte built by his finance minister, the young Louis planned his opulent *château* well west of the city. He changed the very landscape to create his gardens, and installed an elaborate system of pumps to bring water from the Seine to his fountains and pools.

More than 1,000 members of court lived in the attic rooms, and life here was as far removed from the life outside the palace walls as they could make it. Such daily events as 'the King's Rise' took on momentous importance for the coterie.

Although revolutionary outrage emptied the castle of most of the furnishings, it has slowly been restored and pieces donated by foreign countries or collected and purchased in France have helped to fill out the many rooms in a style which is approaching the original splendour.

In the precise centre of the palace lie the **Royal Apartments**. The small staircase linking the king's sitting room to the queen's was added by Louis XV and his mistress, Madame de Pompadour. Look for the secret passage later used by Louis XVI's wife, Marie Antoinette, to escape the rabble barging through the gates. That escape is the supposed occasion of her infamous reply to the people's cry for bread: 'Let them eat cake' (*Qu'ils mangent de la brioche*). Historians cast doubt on whether she used those precise words, but certainly the sentiment is clear. Poverty and suffering were, perhaps, beyond her imagination, just as the opulence that she took for granted is beyond our own.

The **Hall of Mirrors** was used as a royal reception and ballroom. More recently, the Treaty of Versailles ending World War I was signed here. Another historic event, which the French are less wont to recall, took place here in 1871: the proclamation of the German Empire. The pint-size **Opera House**, which was built for Louis XV, is a sumptuous hall which once again welcomes special performances, thanks to recent restoration.

Outdoors, the park was designed by André le Nôtre, who created the image of the royal garden *à la française*. Three more residences dot the landscape. The **Grand Trianon** (open from 10am; closed lunchtime in winter), on the bank of the Grand Canal, was built by Louis XIV. He sought peace

Statues everywhere

within its pink marble walls, away from the crowd at court. The **Petit Trianon** (open from 10am; closed lunchtime in winter) was built by his successor, but mainly enjoyed by the last of the Louis, the ill-fated Louis XVI. Queen Marie Antoinette preferred **Le Hameau**, a make-believe hamlet, where she played milkmaid with fine porcelain milk pails.

In the form of a *fleur-de-lys* (symbol of royalty), the **Grand Canal** stretches out from the foot of the terrace, dividing the wooded park in two. The two large fountains in the central alley are the **Latona** and **Apollo** fountains. The first is a weird amphibian allegory dominating the *tapis vert*, the central lawn. The second represents the god driving a chariot led by powerful horses.

Both sides of the park are studded with groves, ponds, exotic bushes and ancient trees and velvety smooth grass. The fountains are so numerous that even a king's coffers couldn't keep them going nowadays, but on the first and third Sundays of June through September, all gush again, their musical splashing joining birdsong. Occasional evening festivities come complete with fireworks and multi-coloured lights.

9. Chartres

Mostly visited for its Gothic cathedral, Chartres is a pleasant and relaxing place to explore. A world away from the big-city mentality of Paris, Chartres is just 60 miles (97 km) southwest, an hour's train ride from Montparnasse station.

The medieval town of Chartres sits upon a plateau hemmed in by wheat fields on the banks of the river Eure. The spires of the **cathedral** rise high above the rich plain, welcoming pilgrims since the 13th century. It is a short walk uphill from the SNCF train station to the site.

View of the cathedral

The cathedral is a near-perfect example of Gothic architecture, but perhaps its most famous features are the **Rose Windows**. Their fame is due to both their beauty and their age, for they date from the 12th and 13th centuries and are among the oldest examples of this type of religious art to be found in the world. They survived a disastrous fire in 1149, in which most of the previous Romanesque cathedral was destroyed, and the French Revolution. During both world wars they were removed and put into safe keeping.

The 'Chartres blue' in the glass is a rich, deep tone that is not found elsewhere and apparently cannot be duplicated. Some of the panes seem lighter in colour than others, the result of an experimental restoration. Light passing through colours the floor, joining the traces of the ancient marble **Labyrinth** set in the nave. The Labyrinth is symbolic of Christian pilgrimages of the early Middle Ages.

Visit the **Crypt** to see the site of an even more ancient ritual. The cathedral was built on the grounds of a former Druidic worshipping place. You can see a wall of ancient paintings dating from Gallo-Roman times (4th century). Guided tours of the largest and one of the most beautiful crypts in France start from the Maison des Clercs, opposite the south side of the cathedral.

As you leave the cathedral, look up at the two Romanesque towers. The left tower, though known as the 'New Tower', is actually the older, but the delicate Gothic spire atop was added on later, in the 16th century. The thicker spire on the right tower is from the earlier Romanesque period. Here is a good opportunity to observe the difference between these two styles of architecture, both widely present in France.

Behind the cathedral is the former Bishop's Palace, now that **Musée des Beaux Arts**, housing a collection of tapestries, enamels and paintings from the Renaissance through the 18th century. There is also a room devoted to the history of the town. Below the terraced garden behind the museum runs the Eure. It travels past the **Eglise Saint André**, a deconsecrated Romanesque church that is used for concerts. Follow the pathway along the river, past the traditional wash houses and the remains of the old city wall, all the way to the **Place Saint Pierre**, where another set of magnificent stained-glass windows awaits you in the abbey church.

Most of the old town is a protected site, and has been well restored. It is also a lively agricultural centre and capital of the Beauce region. You can tour the city with a guide. Information, maps, books and brochures are available at the tourist office on Rue du Cloître Notre-Dame, alongside the cathedral.

Rose window, Chartres cathedral

This suggestion for a day trip takes you into Normandy, whose peaceful fields and forests lie just a short distance northwest of Paris. Add adventure to your trip by setting out on a bicycle; SNCF French railways offer rentals right at the station. However you go, take a deep breath of the fragrant countryside.

It's a little more difficult to reach **Giverny** than the previous destinations, but nevertheless it is well worth the effort. Take a train from the Gare St Lazare to Vernon, with a journey time of about an hour. At the station, you can take a taxi or hop on a bike for the trip to **Claude Monet's House and Garden** at Giverny (1 April to 31 October only 10am–6pm, closed Monday). The pink and green house itself is an explosion of colour. The dining room, for example, is bright yellow, and the walls are covered with priceless chinaware plates. The kitchen is a soaring sky blue. The walls of the artists' rooms are hung with Japanese prints from his extensive collection.

The gardens are Monet's paintings come to life – or his paintings are his gardens come to art. Here are the waterlilies, the Japanese bridge, the willow and the pond – so many of the subjects of his Impressionist works. Not far away is the **Musée Américain** (1 April to 31 October only 10am–6pm, closed Monday), which charts the impact which Monet and the other Impressionists made on American art.

Giverny is very popular on summer afternoons, so start out early on a weekday to get the most pleasure from your visit. The Seine meets the river Epte here, and there are pretty spots for picnics. If you have a car, continue northwest to **Lyons la Forêt**, a village set in a beech-tree forest. Potted geraniums decorate the windows of typical Normandy half-timbered facades. Otherwise, there are a couple of decent restaurants in Vernon itself.

Monet's house at Giverny

11. Disneyland Paris

Disneyland Paris (open year round; hours are seasonal but generally 10am–6pm, until 8pm on Saturday; 9am–11pm July and August), is the second overseas location for Disney outside the US – the other is in Tokyo, Japan. It is situated at Marne la Vallée 32km (20 miles) east of Paris and can be reached by either car or RER line A from central Paris at Auber, Châtelet or Étoile. Marne-la-Vallée is also linked up to the high-speed TGV and there is a Eurostar train direct from London's Waterloo station.

Disneyland Paris located on this site because of its centrality within Europe: potential venues in the UK and Spain were discounted because of more difficult access. French reaction to the arrival of Disney was mixed – even though Disney researchers had identified Walt himself as originating from the town of Isigny (D'Isigny = Disney).

Huge though the park is, it is still being developed, and in its final form this dream-world will cover an area one-fifth the size of Paris. In the first year of operation, twice as many people visited Disneyland Paris as climbed the Eiffel Tower or visited the Louvre. Even so, these numbers were lower than Disney had hoped, and some plans were rescheduled. Now, however, the park has been deemed a success by all. The park's official language is English, but French is widely spoken.

The gang

Entrance fees vary according to the season, and families with children should consider spreading their visit over two days. Disneyland Paris *passeports* are available in Paris at FNAC stores, the tourist office, the Disney store and Virgin Megastore. To make reservations in one of Disneyland Paris's six hotels, telephone Paris 01 60306053 or the UK number 0990 030303. The on-site hotels can be expensive, but guests get earlier access to the attractions.

Disneyland Paris is similar to its US sisters. Disney's 'imagineers' have created five worlds: Fantasyland; Discoveryland; Main Street USA represents the early 1900s with ragtime and Dixieland bands; Wild West Frontierland; Adventureland has characters like Captain Hook and *Treasure Island*'s Ben Gunn; futuristic Discoveryland has Space Mountain and several attractions with a French theme, such as Les Mystères de Nautilus, an underwater trip 20,000 Leagues Under the Sea that pays homage to French science-fiction writer Jules Verne. The rides and re-creations are very exciting, and 'animatronics' – bringing inanimate objects to life – features highly. Even queuing here can be great entertainment.

Duty Free Regulations

US residents may take back $400 worth of merchandise per traveller for personal use or as gifts, before paying a flat 10 percent tax on additional value up to $1,000. Included in this allowance is 1 litre of alcohol per traveller over the age of 21 and one bottle of US-trademarked perfume. There is no tax on art or antiques more than 100 years old. Families may pool their declarations, provided that no similar ones have been made in the preceding 30-day period. Canadian residents have a $300 yearly limit, in addition to the 50 cigars, 200 cigarettes, 2lbs of tobacco and 40oz of alcohol they may bring in tax free.

European Union (EU) countries have an open border policy, which will eventually be accompanied by the standardisation of VAT. Meanwhile, prices (particularly for alcohol and cigarettes) are remarkably different in neighbouring countries. This has resulted in a fair amount of informal import and export, and has encouraged the black-market sale of goods, particularly alcohol, in the UK.

Technically there is no limit to the amount of goods you can bring into the UK from France, but all the goods must be for personal consumption. If this is the case, then you may pass through the blue channel at customs and no further tax is paid unless the goods were bought tax-free, in which case limits remain fairly low. The term 'for personal use' is interpreted as being a maximum of 800 cigarettes, 400 cigarillos, 200 cigars, 1kg of smoking tobacco, 10 litres of spirits, 20 litres of fortified wines, 90 litres of wine, and 110 litres of beer. If you want to go over this limit to buy wine, say, for a wedding, it is advisable to take documentation to back up your story.

No animals or pets may be brought into the UK without quarantine – and this rule is strictly enforced.

Paris style

Window shopping

Duty free outlets – for instance those at the Eurostar terminal, in airports and on planes and boats – are not always the cheapest places to shop. The mark-up, which can be as much as 100–200 percent, can sometimes overwhelm the tax savings, and you may find you would have been better off getting your duty-free goods from a regular shop in town. At this point you will have to decide whether it is worth reclaiming the duty that will be included in the price.

Only certain shops offer an instant refund on tax. In addition to Galeries Lafayette and Printemps department stores, **Raoul & Curly** at 47 Avenue de l'Opera offers this service. To get the refund you will need to take your plane ticket and passport to the shop to prove you are taking the goods out of the country.

The other alternative is to get the VAT (TVA in France) refunded at the airport. To qualify for this procedure, your purchases in a single store must amount to 1,200 Francs for non-EU residents. The store must fill out a special form (make sure it corresponds to your place of residence). You must include banking information on the form, because refunds are only paid directly into accounts. Customs officials will ask for the forms as you leave, and they will look at the goods, so be sure to allow plenty of time. In general, it is not worth the hassle to seek a refund this way, unless you've got an expensive item to declare.

Alcohol and Perfumes

If you want to buy **alcohol**, I suggest you stick with liqueurs, aperitifs or champagnes. Good wine may suffer in the journey and end up disappointing you. French wine is so competitively priced around the world that you'd do better to buy back home. Major supermarkets have the best prices and a satisfactory selection; luxury shops on the Place de la Madeleine offer high-quality items in gift packages. **Perfumes** are another favourite purchase, but the prices are only interesting if you are able to purchase them tax-free.

Fashion is synonymous with Paris, and just looking at Parisians makes you want to dress up. The venerable couture houses are on Avenue Montaigne and Faubourg St Honoré. For ready-to-wear designer fashion, head for Les Trois Quartiers shopping centre on Boulevard de la Madeleine (Metro Madeleine) where the boutiques of Kenzo, Dorothée Bis, Gentleman Givenchy, etc. offer duty-free facilities. Less classic and more affordable clothes can be found around Saint Germain and the streets around Saint Sulpice where, alongside the prêt-à-porter boutiques of up-and-coming designers, are international  chains such as Gap and shops selling fashionable items for the home.

Les Halles has a wide selection of shops, including a good selection of teenage fashion. Nearby Rue du Jour has dozens of shops selling new and used clothing for men and women.

Look for *Soldes*, seasonal sales often held in January and July. *Liquidation* means 'everything must go'. Women's and men's clothes are sized from 36 (small) to 48 (extra large). Shoes start at 36 (English size 5) through 46 (English size 12). Children's clothes are marked by age, but sizes tend to be less generous than in the UK; baby shoes start at 19. My advice, of course, is to try things on, and any shop will accommodate this request to *essayer*.

To find everyday items that you need while travelling, whether shampoo, a warm sweater, an insole for your shoe, or a sketch pad for your drawings, try one of the many branches of the less expensive department stores **Monoprix, Uniprix** or **Prisunic**. These stores are very handy, located all over town, smaller and less crowded than the major department stores. Most also offer shoe and clothing repair services and have one floor of grocery items. Clean, inexpensive and well-organised, these stores offer good quality merchandise and are pleasant to shop in.

While you can find many **beauty care products** in these stores, smaller specialised boutiques offer more sophisticated products and perfumes as well as services like manicure, hair removal, facial massage etc in their **Salons de Beauté**.

Hairdressers are easy enough to locate, but always busy. One of the most popular salons is **Jacques Dessanges**, with several locations in the city. Call the Franklin Roosevelt salon, tel: 01 43593397, for information and an appointment. Another favourite is **Jean Louis David** (tel: 01 43598208), who has 14 salons and a beauty school with discount prices on modern styles.

The more exclusive **Maniatis** has three salons: 18 Rue Marbeuf (tel: 47233014) near the Champs Elysées, and 35 Rue de Sèvres (tel: 01 45441639) and 12 Rue du Four (tel: 01 46347983), both near St Germain des Prés.

Fun Souvenirs

The Boutique **Chic et Choc** in Les Halles Metro station takes the cake. They have all sorts of items with the Paris Metro logo. Another special spot is the **Réunion des Musées Nationaux**, 10 Rue de l'Abbaye, near St Germain-des-Prés. They offer posters and catalogues from Paris museums, dating back to 1966, and scarves, handbags and jewellery inspired by the great collections. On a higher price scale, try the **Louvre des Antiquaires**, 2 Place du Palais Royal, for antique furnishings, prints and paintings. Some of the dealers here have less expensive shops elsewhere, so ask for a card.

Adventurous visitors will head for **Flea Markets** to dig out something unique. The most well-known is the Puces de Saint-Ouen at **Porte de Clignancourt** (Saturday to Monday 7am–7.30pm; Metro: Porte de Clignancourt). In the city, try the **Marché d'Aligre**, a food and flower market which also has a section of old books, clothes, glassware, lace and jewellery (Place d'Aligre, near Bastille, Metro: Ledru-Rollin; closed Monday). Of the markets outside the city, the best for bargains is the **Marché de Montreuil** to the east (Metro: Porte de Montreuil). Old clothes, junk, and genuine finds all day Saturday, Sunday and Monday.

A few other suggestions for take-homes that you can pick up and pack easily: perfumed soaps in decorative boxes (look in the pharmacy windows); chocolates and other sweet-meats in pretty packets, sold in bakeries and *confiseries*, mustard and vinegar assortments in attractive jars and bottles; 'Perfumes of Paris' collections with sample sizes of an assortment of scents, on sale in many of the smaller beauty product boutiques.

The only problem with shopping in Paris is deciding when to stop and how much your can afford to spend. But even Uncle Scrooge could cough up for a pair of Eiffel Tower earrings (10 to 50 Francs in souvenir shops) or a sachet of lavender to perfume the linen closet (10 to 30 Francs, in department stores).

Preparing for a closer look

Eating Out

It would take years to sample all the restaurants in Paris, and a staff to keep up with changes and openings. Parisians enjoy eating out of their favourite *bistro* as much as discovering a new restaurant or having a night out in a really fine establishment. Take the suggestions given in each itinerary in this book, or walk into a place that looks (and smells) great, or just try the restaurants listed below. Addresses include the *code postale*, of which the last two numbers indicate the district (*arrondissement*). Prices are based on the set price menu, if there is one, or a three-course *à la carte* meal for one person, with a moderately-priced wine.

Many restaurants close on Sunday. Reservations are required in expensive restaurants, and highly recommended on Friday and Saturday nights for moderate restaurants.

The price of dinner may vary, especially if you order a special bottle of wine or champagne. Lunch is served from noon until about 2pm. Dinner service starts around 8pm. *Brasseries* serve a limited menu (eggs, hot ham sandwiches, sausages) all day; cafés generally have cold sandwiches on crusty *baguettes* of bread at any hour. If you want a super gourmet experience, try lunchtime, rather than dinner, when many expensive places have set menus that can offer real savings over *à la carte*.

One of the joys of Paris

Expensive Restaurants

Dinner with a moderately priced wine costs at least 700 Francs per person. Lunch tends to be much cheaper, especially for set menus.

TAILLEVENT
15 Rue Lamennais (75008)
Tel: 01 44951501
Credit cards: American Express, Diner's, Mastercard, Visa
Fine French cuisine in wood-panelled surroundings. This is one of the best restaurants in Paris. Exceptional wine list. Around 900 Francs per person.

LA TOUR D'ARGENT
15 Quai de la Tournelle (75005)
Tel: 01 43542331
Closed on Monday, credit cards: American Express, Mastercard, Diner's Club and Visa
Famous for the view of Notre Dame as well as recipes based on duck. The service is impeccable, the décor divine. Dinner, minimum 900 Francs.

LASSERRE
17 Ave Franklin Roosevelt (75008)
Tel: 01 43595343
Closed on Sunday, Monday and in August, no credit cards accepted
In the summer, you dine under the stars when they roll back the roof up-

Dress up for this one

stairs. There is an incredible wine list, and the dishes are rather on the delicate side. Just using the cutlery is half the pleasure of dining here. Around 800 Francs per head.

ARPEGE
84 Rue de Varenne (75007)
Tel: 01 45514733
Closed Saturday, Sunday lunch, and the middle two weeks of August, credit cards: American Express, Diner's Club, Mastercard and Visa
This superb restaurant is among the top 12 in Paris. The wine-cellar is particularly good, and not expensive. Expect to pay between 500 and 900 Francs, excluding wine.

There's good food everywhere

Moderate Restaurants

There is an abundance of restaurants in this category, where a meal for one with wine costs between 200 and 350 Francs. Here are a few favourites:

TERMINUS NORD
23 Rue de Dunkerque (75010)
Tel: 01 42850515
Open daily, 11am–12.30am, credit cards: American Express, Diner's Club, Mastercard and Visa
Just across from the *Gare du Nord* station, this big, busy brasserie has a 1925 décor and a staff of very professional waiters. It specialises in traditional French food and hearty portions. First-rate seafood, and excellent beef and lamb dishes.

LE BAR DES THÉATRES

6 Ave Montaigne (75008)
Tel: 01 47233463
Open daily, credit card: Visa

This busy, noisy place has been around for over 40 years, serving tasty and traditional French food in a friendly atmosphere. It has its drawbacks: don't mind the napkins, and keep away if you hate cigarette smoke while you're eating. However, on the positive side, this place typifies the kind of restaurant that used to make people say it was just about impossible to get a bad meal in France.

AUBERGE DE JARENTE

7 Rue de Jarente (75004)
Tel: 01 42774935
Closed Sunday, Monday and in August, credit cards: American Express, Diner's Club and Visa

A small but welcoming restaurant specialising in the kind of uncomplicated cuisine that makes a welcome change from some French establishments. Both the *piperade de St Jean* and the *gâteau Basque* can be recommended.

LA CITROUILLE

10 Rue Grégoire de Tours (75006)
Tel: 01 43299041
Open daily

Located in the heart of the Latin Quarter on the famous Left Bank near Odéon, this restaurant serves excellent fresh salads and simple but well-prepared dishes at very reasonable prices. Come here for a pleasant escape from steak and French fries!

Look for the specials

CHEZ PIERROT

18 Rue Etienne Marcel (7502)
Tel: 01 45080548

Located near Les Halles. Known for its good pâtés and wines, excellent French cooking and friendly service. Good value.

CHEZ MA COUSINE

12 Rue Norvins (75018)
Tel: 01 46064935
Open daily, credit cards: American Express, Diner's Club, Mastercard and Visa

Located in Montmartre, right on the Place du Tertre, this small and friendly restaurant also offers a cabaret in the evening. If you want faster food, it has a *crêpe* stand on the street that serves the passing traffic.

Inexpensive Restaurants

For around 180 Francs per person, you can have the pleasure of a good French meal with wine at the following establishments:

CHARTIER

7 Rue du Faubourg Montmartre (75009)
Tel: 01 47708629
Closed Sunday

Located near the Opéra, this is the best-known low-price eatery in town. The ambience is an experience in itself: there is turn-of-the-century decor; the waiters are snappy and the tables are shared; and there is plenty of *bonhommie*. Arrive before 2pm in the afternoon or 9.30 at night, or you probably won't get a seat.

POLIDOR

41 Rue Monsieur-le-Prince (75006)
Tel: 01 43269534
No credit cards

Favoured by students and professors, this Latin Quarter hangout offers home-style cooking and art-deco design. Everything is very relaxed, including the service, and no gastronomic miracles are in order, but Hemingway ate here, and so can you.

PASTAVINO
59 Rue Dauphine (75006)
and 30 Rue Passy (75016)
This Italian restaurant and take-away serves salads, pasta dishes and tasty desserts at unbeatable prices. More branches will be opening.

LE TEMPS DES CERISES
131 Rue de la Cerisaie (75004)
Tel: 01 42720863
Modest family-run restaurant in the Marais by the Bastille. Simple working men's food. Excellent value. Lunch only. Closed Saturday, Sunday and in August.

CAFÉ DE LA MAIRIE
8 Place St-Sulpice (75006)
Left Bank eaterie undiscovered by most tourists. A genuine piece of France. No credit cards.

Bars and Wine Bars

LE RUBIS
10 Rue du Marché St Honoré (75001)
Closed on weekends and in August
No credit cards
This is the place to be when the *Beaujolais Nouveau* comes out in October and the party that assembles fills up the whole street. At other times of the year, it is a pleasant place for lunch with a glass of something divine. Popular *plats du jour* include *boeuf bourguignon* and lentils with salt pork (*petit salé aux lentilles*).

L'ECLUSE
15 Quai des Grands-Augustins (75006)
Rue Mondétour (75001)
Rue du Pont Lodi (75006)
Place de la Madeleine (75008)

Drink in the sun

Rue François 1er (75008)
All branches are closed on Sunday
L'Ecluse is the grand-daddy of all Parisian wine bars, and so far its popularity shows no signs of diminishing. Although it is a comparatively expensive place, it offers a truly outstanding selection of Bordeaux wines, served by the glass and the bottle, plus a range of appetising snacks to accompany them.

BRASSERIE DE L'ILLE ST LOUIS
53 Quai de Bourbon (75004
Tel: 0143540209
Lively Alsation brasserie. Closed during August.

HARRY'S NEW YORK BAR
5 Rue Daunou (75002)
I couldn't leave this one out. Harry's opened in 1911, was virtually a second home to Hemingway (as were many bars in Paris!), and the Bloody Mary was created here. Harry's is still popular today, attracting plenty of interesting characters. You can linger on here until the wee small hours.

Nightlife

There is plenty to do in Paris after the street-lights blink on. Expect a late start in summer.

River tours: The **Vedettes du Pont Neuf**, entrance under the Pont Neuf off Place Dauphine, leave roughly every 30 minutes until 5pm Monday to Thursday, and until 10pm the rest of the week. The trip takes about an hour and powerful spotlights illuminate the bridges and buildings as you go. The same tours are run by **Bateaux Mouches** at Pont d'Alma, although less frequently. Across from the Eiffel Tower at the Pont d'Iéna are **Les Bateaux Parisiens**, who also offer gastronomic cruises.

Nocturnal bus tours: These pass the spendidly illuminated monuments of the city. Some end at the Moulin Rouge for French can-can and champagne, or the Lido on the Champs-Elysées. Two well-known tours in town are **Paris Vision** (214 Rue de Rivoli 75001) and **Cityrama** (4 Place des Pyramides 75001); their packages are also sold in many agencies, and most hotels carry their leaflets. The companies also organise day trips to popular sites such as Versailles, Giverny, Disneyland Paris and Chartres.

Stage: Tickets to the ballet, opera, concerts, or theatre productions can be bought at an agency or at the theatre

itself. The FNAC stores (music and books) around town (there's a main branch in the Forum des Halles shopping centre) sell tickets to most concerts. For theatrical productions, go to the Kiosque de la Madeleine, a big ticket booth in the middle of Place de la Madeleine. You can buy half-price tickets on the day.

Complete weekly listings are in *L'Officiel des Spectacles*, *Pariscope* and other magazines. Also look out for Paris's distinctive green 'Morris Columns', on street corners, which are usually splashed with posters.

See Paris by night

Jazz clubs

Paris loves jazz, and the clubs seem to have undergone a renaissance recently. Check the listings in the magazine *L'Officiel des Spectacles* to see what's on in the following clubs.

NEW MORNING
7–9 Rue des Petits Ecuries (75010)
Big, scant décor, tucked in a back alley. Some greats keep coming back, including Richie Havens, Taj Mahal, Wayne Shorter, Stan Getz and Prince. Informal and hip. (Tel: 01 45235141.)

JAZZ CLUB LIONEL HAMPTON
Hotel Meridien
81 Blvd Gouvion-St Cyr (75017)
A favourite with performers and fans. Seats several hundred. Run by a local jazz hero known simply as Moustache, who shows some of the finest jazz musicians, such as Harry Edison, Oscar Peterson, Memphis Slim and Benny Carter the respect they deserve. Not a night owl? Enjoy jazz here on Sunday, over brunch.

LE PETIT JOURNAL
71 Blvd St Michel (75005) and
LE PETIT JOURNAL MONTPARNASSE
13 Rue du Commandant-Mouchotte (75014)
Same owners, but different styles. The St Michel version features Dixieland and Swing, the Montparnasse version has contemporary names like Herbie Hancock, Art Blakey and Stéphane Grappelli. Good food and good vibes.

After-Hours Clubs

Clubs in Paris tend to be very 'clubby' subjecting would-be partiers to heavy scrutiny at the door. Dress fashionably, and bring plenty of money.

LES BAINS
7 Rue du Bourg-l'Abbé (75003)
Old public bath house, the gathering place of fashion victims and the young and hip. To be sure of getting in, make a reservation to eat at the restaurant first (Tel: 01 48870180).

LE TANGO
13 Rue au Maire (75003)
Meeting place for African *sapeurs*, guys who spend fantastic sums of money on incredible clothes. You have a wild time in store, if you're dressed right!

LE NEO
21 Rue Montorgeuil (75001)
A cellar club that attracts a mix of customers on its varied evenings.

CASTEL
15 Rue Princess (75006)
A cellar club that attracts a mix of customers on its varied evenings.

A night out

Calendar of Special Events

The main tourist season in Paris is from June through September, and Easter is also a very busy period. July and August are big holiday months for the French, so a number of shops, restaurants and theatres are closed. However, there is still plenty for visitors to do, including summer festivals, sound and light shows, and fireworks displays, and there is a happy and relaxed atmosphere in the city streets, which are less crowded than at other times of the year.

National holidays involve closed banks and heavy traffic, so plan around the following: **1 January, Easter Monday, 1 May (Labour Day), 8 May (VE Day), Ascension Day, Pentecost (Whit Monday), 14 July, 15 August (Assumption), 1 November (All Saints' Day), 11 November (Armistice), 25 December**.

When packing seasonable clothes for your holiday, keep in mind that the French, and especially Parisians, dress up to go to work, out to dinner, or to the theatre. Jeans are fine for visiting museums, but frowned upon in many restaurants and expensive shops.

The Tour de France passes through

National colours on Bastille Day

JANUARY – MARCH

The weather is cold and damp, and the only advantages of this period are lower fares and hotel rates, and thinner crowds at the museums.

APRIL – MAY

Springtime in Paris is a legend, of course, and one the city usually lives up to, if only for a fleeting moment. Temperatures lie in the range 60–70°F (16–22°C). The days lengthen deliciously as heavy chestnut blooms appear against unfurling green foliage. If you are lucky with your timing, Paris in these months can be at its most enchanting.

The sporting highlights include the Paris Marathon in April and the French Open Tennis Championship at the end of May.

JUNE – JULY

In the early part of the summer there are many celebrations. The Festival du Marais presents concerts, theatre and dance in some of the neighbourhood's lovely old buildings and churches, as well as special events held in major halls. This more than makes up for annual closings. Other musical events include the Montmartre Jazz Festival and a series of classical concerts at the Sorbonne.

The 14 July is Bastille Day, known in France as La Fête Nationale. The party begins with a morning military parade down the Champs Elysées, continues with fireworks over the Eiffel Tower and dancing till dawn at the various Firemen's Balls. Watch out for sizzling firecrackers!

The Tour de France bicycle race sprints to a finish on the Champs Elysées around the end of the fourth week of July.

AUGUST

The city slows down into a holiday atmosphere. Visit the fair in the Tuileries Park and go on the big Ferris wheel for a thrilling view.

SEPTEMBER

This period is called *la rentrée* – the return. There are: new fashions; a major art show, the Foire Internationale de l'Art Contemporain (FIAC); plus new productions in theatre, music, dance and film in the Paris Autumn Festival, running through December.

OCTOBER – NOVEMBER

October is wine month, with the Montmartre harvest festival and the arrival of Beaujolais Nouveau. It is also time for the Prix de l'Arc de Triomphe; and the Paris–Deauville vintage car run. The International Dance Festival continues through November.

DECEMBER

Christmas shopping starts at the end of November, and the streets are magnificent. The city has a bustling, busy quality in the days preceding the end-of-the-year holidays. Christmas is a family affair, but New Year's Eve is a big party occasion.

Practical Information

GETTING THERE

By Plane

You could arrive at one of two airports serving Paris. **Charles de Gaulle** (tel: 01 48622280), also referred to as 'Roissy', is the bigger and more modern of the two. From there, you can take the RER line B to the Gare du Nord (every 15 minutes) or the Air France bus to the Arc de Triomphe. The Roissybus runs roughly every 15 minutes, 6am–11pm, between the airport and the Place de l'Opéra, taking about 45 minutes. A taxi takes about 40–50 minutes to reach the centre, and costs about 220 Francs. Add another 30 minutes for a rush-hour journey.

Orly is the other major Parisian airport (tel: 01 49751515), to the south of Paris, and it handles mostly domestic flights and charter flights. Air France buses travel between Orly and the Invalides Terminal. This is a convenient drop-off place, where you can board either the Metro or RER directly. The Air France buses then continue on to Gare Montparnasse.

A city bus (Orlybus) comes into the southern end of Paris at the Denfert-Rochereau Metro station every 15 minutes. A taxi takes 30-40 minutes (but much longer during rush hour), and costs about 150 Francs.

By Train

Eurostar: since the opening of the Channel Tunnel in 1995 it has been possible to travel by rail between central London (Waterloo) and central Paris (Gare du Nord) in just three hours.

Various special tickets and cheap deals are offered on the Eurostar service: ask what is available when you make your booking. In theory, tickets can be booked up to 30 minutes before departure; but in practice the cheap tickets (especially at the weekend, even in the low season) get booked up early.

Check-in closes 20 minutes before the train leaves. For more information and to make bookings, contact Eurostar, tel: 0345 303030.

Gare St Lazare

Visas

Travellers to France must have a valid passport. EU and American citizens do

Cash supplier

not need visas, but visitors from other countries should contact the nearest French consulate or a local tourist office.

Time

France is six hours ahead of US Eastern Standard time and one hour ahead of Greenwich Mean Time.

Electricity

Paris runs on 220 volts, 50 cycles. If you carry a travel iron or hair dryer, make sure you have an adaptor so that it will fit in the French socket. If you've forgotten to bring one along, you can buy one from an 'Electricité' or 'Quincaillerie' (hardware) shop.

MONEY MATTERS

Many banks in Paris will change cash or traveller's cheques, and there are no special differences in rates. Banking hours are 9am–4.30pm on weekdays. The exchange window at the Gare du Nord is open until midnight on weekdays, and other station banks are open until 8pm.

Automatic exchange machines at the Opéra (the BNP Bank) and at No 66 on the Champs Elysées (BRED) will convert foreign bills into Francs. The easiest way to draw cash is to use your credit or cashpoint/ATM card in the ATMs outside most banks. The instructions are generally in English. Avoid changing money at hotels, where exchange rates may be poor.

Hotline numbers for lost cards: American Express (tel: 01 47777200); Diners Club (tel: 01 49061725); Carte Bleu/Visa (tel: 01 42771190).

The basic unit of money is the Franc, divided into 100 Centimes. Coins are worth 5, 10, 20 or 50 Centimes; 1, 2, 5, 10 or 20 Francs. Notes are worth 20, 50, 100, 200 or 500 Francs.

Tipping

Tipping is common in a number of places. In hotels, restaurants and cafés there is always a service charge, but people usually leave the small change from the bill in the saucer. Prices listed *prix nets* or *service compris* mean service is included. If the price says *service en sus* or *service non compris*, an extra 12–15 percent will be added to the total. A 5 Franc tip is usually given to: room service waiters (except breakfast), ushers, washroom and cloakroom attendants. Taxi drivers and hairdressers expect about 15 percent.

GETTING AROUND

Paris has 20 *arrondissements* (districts) spiralling out from the Louvre. The last two numbers of the postal code (750XX) are the *arrondissement* number.

The Metro

Metro, Buses and Trains

In the Metro, ask for a free map (*un plan du Métro*) and a copy of the public transportation guide *Paris Patchwork*. There is also a plan of the central section of the Metro on page 101 of this guide.

You can travel on bus and Metro with tickets purchased at the ticket booth in any Metro station. These are much cheaper when you buy 10 at once (*un carnet*). There is also a tourist card called *Paris*

Visite, available for foreign visitors and valid for two to five days of unlimited travel on the Metro, bus (including airports), RER and suburban SNCF lines and Montmartre funicular. There are two types of *Paris Visite* available: for zones 1–3 or for zones 1–5 (the latter stretches as far as Versailles and Disneyland Paris). The ticket also gives discount admission to many sites.

Another useful option for visitors is *Formule 1*, which is valid for one day and allows unlimited journeys by metro, RER, SNCF suburban trains and bus.

It is simple to use the **Metro** system, which is the densest in the world with stops, on average, every 550 metres (180ft) or so. The lines are named after their terminal points, for example Château de Vincennes-Pont de Neuilly crosses the city from east to west, ending at those two stops. You can transfer as many times as you need to on the same ticket, by following the orange signs marked *Correspondances* in the tunnels.

In general, the Metro is quite safe, although you should guard your wallet or purse carefully, especially when surrounded by big crowds.

Trains run from 5.30am–12.30am. Follow the sign *Accés aux Quais* to reach the tracks, and *Sortie* to the street. Keep hold of your ticket until you exit the system: it may be checked by inspectors.

Buses run on different schedules, but usually start around 6.30am and stop around 8.30pm. Only certain buses run on Sunday or late at night. Bus shelters all have maps and route information, and if you board a bus you must show your pass or punch a ticket in the machine by the driver. Check the route map to see how many bus zones you will be going through, if more than two, you must punch two tickets.

If you can decipher public transport systems, the city buses are a great way to get around, even though they are not as fast as the Metro. At least you see Paris

from the buses. The Balabus is particularly good for sightseeing, with ten stops (marked *Bb*) between Gare du Lyon and La Grande Arche de La Défense.

The RER lines are rapid transit lines that go out to the suburbs. They can be useful for crossing town quickly, and you can use a Metro ticket on the RER within the city. But to get to Versailles, for example, if you don't have a pass that covers it, you must buy a more expensive ticket, which you will have to insert in a machine to exit the station on arrival.

Taxis

Taxis are best found at taxi stands, clearly marked by large signs. You can also call a taxi company. Alpha Taxi (tel: 01 45858585); Taxis Bleus: (tel: 01 49361010). Both offer 24-hour service. G7 Taxis (tel: 01 47394739) accepts credit cards, minimum 50 Francs.

If you call a taxi, the meter starts running when the driver gets the call. There is an extra charge for luggage,

train-station pick-up, and sometimes authorised rate hikes may be posted in the window. Three passengers is the limit, and cabbies are strict about this rule.

Banks have various hours (see *Money Matters*), generally from 9am–4.30pm Monday to Friday, with some branches closed at lunchtime, and/or on Monday; some open on Saturday.

The **Post Office** is open daily from 8am–7pm and Saturday until noon (for branches with longer hours, see *Communications and News* in this chapter.)

Department stores open 10am–6.30pm, and close on Sunday. Many smaller shops close on Monday (especially food stores) and some on Wednesday. Bakeries and some others close for lunch from about 1–4pm. Most shops open until 7–8pm.

Public offices open 9am–5pm Monday to Friday, and sometimes Saturday morning. They are often closed noon–2pm.

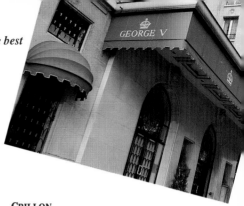

One of the best

ACCOMMODATION

There are many, many hotels in Paris, but it can be hard to find a room at busy periods. Your travel agent can probably book a room for you, otherwise reserve in advance. If you are booking on arrival, visit the Tourist Office on the Champs Elysées (Metro: Charles de Gaulle) or any of the main train stations except St Lazare. For a small fee they find you a room. You can contact the hotels below to make a reservation. Breakfast is usually extra, from 30 Francs. Hotel tax costs from 1 Franc per person per night in unclassified hotels to 7 Francs in luxury hotels.

Deluxe Hotels

A double room with a bath costs at least 2,000 Francs a night.

INTERCONTINENTAL PARIS
3 Rue de Castiglione (75001)
Tel: 01 44771111
Fax: 01 44771460
450 rooms, excellent location, great service, all modern conveniences.

MEURICE
228 Rue de Rivoli (75001)
Tel: 01 44581010
Fax: 01 44581016
180 rooms, modern conveniences in a lovely old building, air conditioning.

RITZ
15 Place Vendôme (75001)
Tel: 01 43163030
Fax: 01 43163178
Everything is perfect. This hotel was the inspiration for the word 'ritzy'. 187 rooms, good restaurants, spacious public rooms, all conveniences, air conditioning and secretarial services.

CRILLON
10 Place de la Concorde (75008)
Tel: 01 44711500
Fax: 01 44711502
163 rooms in a hotel on a fantastic site with views over the River Seine. The hotel is next door to the American Embassy. The Crillon was refurbished in the early 1980s; it has an excellent restaurant and air conditioning.

PLAZA-ATHÉNÉE
25 Ave Montaigne (75008)
Tel: 01 47237833
Fax: 01 47202070
210 sound-proofed rooms and suites in a hotel located near the Champs Elysées. The Plaza Athénée has restaurants, a disco and air conditioning.

GEORGE V
31 Ave George V (75008)
Tel: 01 47235400
Fax: 01 47204000
260 rooms in a completely modern and air-conditioned hotel. The restaurant and the bar are very popular with the international upper-crust – its a place you might see starlets and film agents as well as businessmen.

Expensive Hotels

For a double room with a bath in this grade of hotel you can expect to pay about 850–1,500 Francs.

NORMANDY
7 Rue de l'Echelle (75001)
Tel: 01 42603021
Fax: 01 42604581
115 rooms, all with bathrooms. Restaurant and bar. Comfortable and relaxing place to stay.

DEUX-ILES
59 Rue St Louis-en-L'Ile (75004)
Tel: 01 43261335
Fax: 01 43296025
17 rooms, all with bath or shower in a lovely 17th-century house; peaceful and friendly; bar and sitting room.

ANGLETERRE
44 Rue Jacob (75006)
Tel: 01 42603472
Fax: 01 42601693.
27 rooms, all with bath or shower, in what was once the home of the British Ambassador. Good service, traditional surroundings, central location.

HOLIDAY INN
10 Place de la République (75011)
Tel: 01 43554434
Fax: 01 47003234
One of several Holiday Inns in Paris. 318 rooms, all with bath or shower. Restaurant, bar, air-conditioning.

TERRASS
12–14 Rue Joseph-de-Maistre (75018)
Tel: 01 46067285
Fax: 01 42522911
101 rooms in Montmartre, baths. Restaurant and bar, calm location.

Moderate Hotels

One night in a double room will cost about 250–500 Francs. All the hotels listed have fewer than 100 rooms; some will have bath/shower rooms and some will not.

TIMHOTEL
This new chain has several 2–3-star hotels in town, all well equipped (all rooms have bath), small and friendly. They are all highly recommended and definitely require reservations. Those below are 2-star.

ITALIE
22 Rue Barrault (75013)
Tel: 01 45806767
Fax: 01 45893693

PIGALLE
3 Rue Frochot (75019)
Tel: 01 42853166
Fax: 01 49950221

MONTMARTRE
11 Place Emile Goudeau, Rue Ravignan (75018)
Tel: 01 42557479
Fax: 01 42557101

MONTPARNASSE
22 Rue de l'Arrivée (75015)
Tel: 01 45489662
Fax: 01 45489662

LE LOUVRE
4 Rue Croix des Petits Champs (75001)
Tel: 01 42603486
Fax: 01 42601039

LA BOURSE
3 Rue de la Banque (75002)
Tel: 01 42615390
Fax: 01 42600539

SAINT LAZARE
113 Rue St Lazare (75008)
Tel: 01 43875353
Fax: 01 43876625

Timhotel has a central reservation service: tel: 01 44158115, fax: 01 44159526. American Express, Diners, Mastercard and Visa are accepted.

GRANDES ECOLES
75 Rue du Cardinal Lemoine (75005)
Tel: 01 43267923
Fax: 01 43252815
Not very fancy, but well-located and pleasant, good value.

St Jacques

35 Rue des Ecoles (75005)
Tel: 01 43268253
Fax: 01 43256550
Like the above, an ordinary Parisian hotel, centrally located.

Inexpensive Hotels

This category includes hotels that charge less than 300 Francs a night, of which there are many, particularly near the railway stations. Most are fairly comfortable, but there may be a big difference in price between rooms with and without private bathrooms.

Palais

2 Quai de la Mégisserie (75001)
Tel: 01 42369825
Fax: 01 42214167
19 rooms near the Sainte Chapelle.

Esmeralda

4 Rue St Julien le Pauvre (75005)
Tel: 01 43541920
15 rooms near Notre Dame cathedral in the busy Latin Quarter. Credit cards are not accepted.

Place des Vosges

12 Rue de Birague (75004)
Tel: 01 42726046
Fax: 01 42720264
16 rooms, all with bath or shower, Marais district. Pleasant, small and friendly — book well in advance. Credit cards are accepted.

Palais Bourbon

49 Rue de Bourgogne (75007)
Tel: 01 45516332
Fax: 01 45552021
32 rooms with bath/shower. Small but modern; near the Invalides and the Rodin Museum.

Ask a policeman

If you lose your money, passport or other papers, or if they are stolen, look for the police station (*Commissariat*) nearest the site of theft or loss to make an official declaration before reporting to the embassy of your country. You will need proof of theft or loss in order to claim on your insurance policy.

Ambulance (SAMU)
Tel: 15

Police Emergency
Tel: 17

Fire Department
Tel: 18 (emergency first aid)

Doctor
SOS Médecins
Tel: 01 47077777

American Hospital
Tel: 01 46412525

Franco-British Hospital
Tel: 01 46392222

British and American Pharmacy
1 Rue Auber (75009)
Metro: Opera
8.30am–8pm Monday to Saturday, English spoken.

24-Hour Pharmacy: Dérhy
84 avenue des Champs-Elysées (75008)
Metro: George V
9am–7.30pm Monday to Saturday, English spoken.

SOS-Help
English spoken
Crisis hot line: 01 47238080 from 3–11 pm (subject to change).

COMMUNICATIONS AND NEWS

Post Offices

Post offices are open from 8am–7pm Monday to Friday, and many are open until noon on Saturday. They have distinctive yellow signs with a bird silhouette and the letters PTT. The following branches have extended hours: **Poste Louvre** (52 Rue du Louvre, 75001, Metro: Louvre or Les Halles) is open until midnight Sunday to Thursday and 24 hours on Friday and Saturday; **Poste Paris 8** (71 Ave. des Champs Elysées, 75008, Metro: Franklin Roosevelt) is open 8am–10pm Monday to Saturday, Sunday 10am–noon and 2–8pm for mail only.

Telephones and Telegrams

There are public telephones in all post offices and booths on the street; a café-tabac has a telephone and most ordinary cafés have telephones for the use of customers. In cafés, you may occasionally have to buy a token (*jeton*) at the counter, or pay the cashier directly, or use a coin in the phone. Otherwise, most public phones now take *Télécartes*, plastic cards, which are sold in denominations of 50 units and 120 units, available from tobacconists, post offices and approved vendors (carrying the sticker *Telecarte en vente ici*).

To call other countries, first dial the access code **00**: **Australia** (61); **Germany** (49); **Italy** (39); **Netherlands** (31); **Spain** (34); **UK** (44); **US** and **Canada** (1). If using a US credit phone card, call the company's access number below: AT&T, tel: 00-0011; MCI, tel: 00-0019; Sprint, tel: 00-00874.

Telegrams can be sent from any Post Office. There is a special phone number for telegrams in English: 05334411. **Telefax** services are available at the Louvre Post Office (address above) and at a few branches.

Media and Bookstores

To keep on top of what is happening while you are in town, both *L'Officiel des Spectacles* and *Pariscope* publish an extensive list of restaurants, bars and clubs, concerts, plays and movies in town, information on museums, tours and sports, with hours, addresses and phone numbers.

American and British papers and magazines are available at many news stands too. For further English reading, try these big bookshops:

BRENTANO'S
37 Ave de l'Opéra (75002)
Metro: Opéra

GALIGNANI
224 Rue de Rivoli (75001)
Metro: Tuileries

SHAKESPEARE & CO
37 Rue de la Bûcherie (75005)
Metro: Cité

W H SMITH
248 Rue de Rivoli (75001)
Metro: Concorde

MUSEUMS

The museums of Paris deserve every bit of the praise lavished upon them by visitors from near and far. Check the *Officiel* magazine for current exhibitions and precise information on opening hours (these are subject to change). City of Paris museums close on Monday, national museums on Tuesday, and private museums may close on Tuesday or Friday. There are reductions for students, children under 18, and seniors, so bring along identification if you fit any of these categories. Many national museums are free or half-priced on Sunday. The **Carte Musées** (available in main Metro stations, museums, the tourist office and monuments) gives you

access to over 60 museums and monuments in Paris (including the Louvre, Orsay, Pompidou, Picasso, La Villette, Versailles, Notre Dame...) for 1, 3 or 5 days.

In addition to the museums included in the itineraries in this book, there are many others well worth a visit. Here are a few.

MUSÉE DES ARTS DE LA MODE ET DES ARTS DÉCORATIFS
107 Rue de Rivoli (75001)
Metro: Palais Royal
Within the Louvre building but with a separate entrance, these two museums are well worth a visit. The first presents the history of fashion from the 17th to the 20th centuries; the second displays beautifully crafted furniture, porcelain, crystal and *objets d'art*. Not all the latter collection may be on display while renovation continues.

MUSÉE D'ORSAY
1 Rue de Bellechasse (75007)
Metro: Solférino; RER: Orsay
Open 10am–6pm, from 9am on Sunday and in summer, Thursday until 9.45pm (tickets sold until 8pm). Closed on Monday. The long-abandoned Orsay train station in the centre of Paris was saved from destruction many years ago, but it wasn't given a new purpose until fairly recently.

Preserving the building's *belle époque* architecture, Gae Aulenti redesigned the inner space into several exhibition levels, while keeping all the airy majesty of the original train station. Now it is devoted to works from the last half of the 19th century. One section, showing works by Delacroix and Ingres, leads up to the birth of Impressionism in the 1870s. Witness the changing aesthetics in works by Monet, Manet and Renoir. On the upper level are works by Van Gogh and Cézanne. Exhibitions in the two towers bring us up to the end of the century with Art Nouveau. Do not miss the opulent restaurant.

MUSÉE GREVIN (Waxworks)
10 Blvd Montmartre (75009)
Grand Balcon, Forum des Halles centre
The Montmartre site (Metro: Rue Montmartre) opens daily 1–7pm (last tickets at 6pm), from 10am in school holidays.

The Forum des Halles site (Metro: Les Halles) opens 10.20am–6.45pm on weekdays, and from 1–8pm on Sunday and holidays. Plenty of turn-of-the-century characters and a few present-day stars animate the museums, which are popular with children. There are also magic shows.

MUSÉE D'ART MODERNE DE LA VILLE DE PARIS
11 Ave du Président Wilson (75016)
Metro: Alma-Marceau
Open 10am–5.30pm, weekends until 6.45pm. Closed on Monday. Somewhat neglected and overshadowed by newer museums, this big, echoing place is usually calm, cool and uncrowded on a summer day, a haven from the crowds and the elements. The period of art represented here falls somewhere between Orsay and the Pompidou Centre, Post Impressionism up through Braque and Rouault. One wing now houses the **Musée d'Art et d'Essai** (closed on Tuesday).

USEFUL INFORMATION

Children

There are several babysitting services; I suggest Kid Services (tel: 01 47660052) or Baby Prestige (tel: 01 53530202). Museums that are specially interesting to young travellers are Orsay (interactive computer terminals), Musée de la Marine, La Villette. There is a good children's library in the Pompidou Centre, where older kids can amuse themselves.

Tourist Office, Parisian tourist offices, or from the Comité National Français de Liaison pour la Réadaptation des Handicapés, 263 bis rue de Tolbiac (75007), tel: 01 53806666.

Senior Citizens

Seniors in Paris benefit from many reductions. To do so, they must provide proof of age, and in some cases (for reduced train fares) provide a passport-sized photo which is affixed to a discount card.

Tourist Offices

The main tourist office is at 127 Avenue des Champs Elysées (75008), Metro: Charles de Gaulle-Etoile. There are also branches in airports and train stations (except St Lazare). For information in English, tel: 01 49525354, fax: 01 49525300.

EMBASSIES & CONSULATES

Australia, 4 Rue Jean-Rey (75015), tel: 01 40593300
Canada, 35 Ave Montaigne (75008), tel: 01 44432900
Germany, 13–15 Avenue Franklin D Roosevelt, 75008, tel: 01 53834500
Ireland, 4 Rue Rude (75016), tel: 01 44176700
New Zealand, 7 Rue Léonard-de-Vinci, 75016, tel: 01 45002411
UK, 35 Rue Fbg St Honoré. 75008, tel: 01 42663810
USA, 2 Avenue Gabriel, 75008, tel: 01 43122222

Kids aged 7–11 years can be left in the Jardin des Halles play area at the Forum des Halles while you shop. There are puppet theatres in the Luxembourg Gardens, in the Champs de Mars park next to the Eiffel Tower, and at the Rond Point des Champs Elysées.

A reduction for families (*Familles nombreuses*) is applied in some museums and for train fares at off-peak periods. The booklet *Paris avec des yeux d'enfants*, free from tourist offices, lists Parisian attractions particularly suitable for children.

Students

Students must bring a valid student ID with a photo to be eligible for reductions at museums, theatres, etc. You can get more information on reductions at the Centre d'Information et Documentation Jeunesse (CIDJ), 101 Quai Branly (75015), tel: 01 44491200. Metro: Bir Hakeim.

Another useful address for young travellers is the *Accueil des Jeunes en France*, 119 Rue St Martin (75004). Metro: Rambuteau. They can help you find budget accommodation and suggest where you can meet like-minded people.

Disabled

Disabled travellers will have difficulty using public transport and access to many older buildings is limited. Some efforts are made however, and there is a taxi service for people in wheelchairs, a special bus service for the disabled, and the Louvre museum offers tours for the handicapped (including the blind).

The government publishes a booklet, *Touristes quand même*, which you can pick up in person at the French National

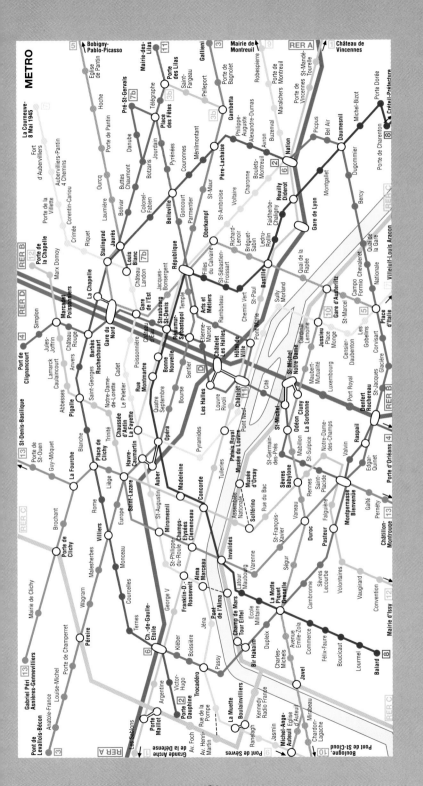

METRO

Index

N, O, P

R, S, T

U, V, W, Z

ACKNOWLEDGMENTS

Photography by

6/7, 10/11	Ping Amranand
17T & B	Archiv Für Kunst und geschichte, Berlin
16, 20, 23T & B, 25, 26T, 30, 31B, 32T, 33, 35, 36, 38T & B, 40T & B, 41, 42, 46T & B, 48T, 50, 53B, 54, 55, 56T, 58T, 59, 61, 63T & B, 64, 65T & B, 66, 67T, 69T, 71, 72, 74, 75T & B, 76, 77T & B, 78, 79, 81, 83, 92, 95, 100T	Guy Bourdíer
13, 18, 22, 29, 34, 39, 47, 48B, 51, 52, 53T, 56B, 60, 68, 69B, 70, 80, 82, 84, 85T & B, 86, 87, 88, 89T & B, 91, 93T & B, 94T & B, 96, 97T & B, 98, 99, 100B, 101	Annabel Elston
12, 15T	Musées de la Ville de Paris
5, 21, 24T & B, 26B, 27, 28, 31T, 32B, 35T, 37, 43T & B, 49, 58B, 67B, 73, 90	Bill Wassman

Handwriting	V Barl
Cover Design	Klaus Geisler
Cartography	Berndtson & Berndtson